T0208399

INJUSTICE
UNDER THE LAW

MARK SCALETTY

INJUSTICE UNDER THE LAW

Copyright © 2024 Mark Scaletty.

All rights reserved. No part of this book may be used or reproduced by any means, graphic, electronic, or mechanical, including photocopying, recording, taping or by any information storage retrieval system without the written permission of the author except in the case of brief quotations embodied in critical articles and reviews.

iUniverse books may be ordered through booksellers or by contacting:

iUniverse
1663 Liberty Drive
Bloomington, IN 47403
www.iuniverse.com
844-349-9409

Because of the dynamic nature of the Internet, any web addresses or links contained in this book may have changed since publication and may no longer be valid. The views expressed in this work are solely those of the author and do not necessarily reflect the views of the publisher, and the publisher hereby disclaims any responsibility for them.

Any people depicted in stock imagery provided by Getty Images are models, and such images are being used for illustrative purposes only.
Certain stock imagery © Getty Images.

ISBN: 978-1-6632-6043-7 (sc)
ISBN: 978-1-6632-6042-0 (e)

Library of Congress Control Number: 2024903157

Print information available on the last page.

iUniverse rev. date: 02/20/2024

OPENING

First let me say that I am not a writer, nor do I play one on television. I suffered an injury at work that cost me almost everything, even my life. What I have written here could educate and warn you about what could and will happen should you get injured.

My disabling injury took over seven long years to get resolved. Many lawyers from different law firms and even the Attorney General were involved. It cost me my wife, my career, my house and over a million dollars.

It's inconceivable that my family, my lawyer, my employer, coworkers and more conspired to ruin me financially, mentally and physically. They used a fake judge, fake stenographers, and even staged court hearings, and almost pulled it off.

This is a non-fiction account of my journey will have you amazed at how the judicial system really works and the tools the lawyers use to work it against you. Along the way of this horrendous trail of deceit, the people hearing my story told me I should write a book, that people won't believe it. So, here you go, read on, but don't let this happen to you.

Mark E. Scaletty

CONTENTS

CHAPTER 1

FIVE YEARS INTO IT

"I'm done! I can't do this anymore. The moving truck will be here Tuesday." My wife told me on a beautiful Saturday afternoon. I couldn't say I blamed her for leaving me. Who would have thought that there could possibly be so much deception involved. My lawyer had staged court hearings and meetings at the Missouri Division of Employment Security with a fake Judge, fake depositions, even a fake stenographer. I wondered how many lawyers, insurance adjusters and judges were in on this million-dollar lawsuit? And what was their take? And the two-week jury trial to be held in Independence, Missouri (2016-CV19063), that was scheduled to start April 17th, 2023! What ever happened with that? The sad part is that I wasn't his only victim, oh no! There were many other individuals and families that were also lied to and deceived by this lawyer rookie with his superiors well involved. Even my daughter, Maria was led to this phony and hung out to dry.

I lost my occupation, my house, my savings and income and then my wife. How could such a preventable injury at work, that left me legally disabled, turn into over a sevenyear fiasco. I even came close to death, thanks to malicious stress that was caused by the deceit and malice of my attorney. I believe he conspired with my employer in various attempts to ensure that I was physically, financially and mentally devastated. This would ensure my million dollar lawsuit never made it to the real court system and keep the public from hearing the truth.

I will demonstrate my findings and the outcome and what they were charged with, but more importantly, how the guilty got away, and how they manipulated the system to keep their wealth and themselves free from prosecution. No one likes lawyers or bosses that are arrogant,

1

condescending jerks. So how did I get so lucky to find a whole mess of these, plus the added characteristic of them being pathological liars.

Seven plus years is a very long time to have to weave through the court system for the same workman's compensation case and same discrimination lawsuit. Most are settled in a year maybe two. But this journey will certainly open your eyes as to how you can be manipulated by your lawyer and your employer and how they will work against you in their interest, not yours. Don't trust that your lawyer is honest or has integrity to do the right thing. Mine didn't. It's a chance you take with any referral. You might wonder, did they get caught for what they did? The short answer is yes, and I was the first client to expose what was going on. But did they get punished? You be the judge this time, not the fictional one they had.

In my case, I went to family, my first cousin, the same age. 'Ricky' when we were youngsters growing up together. But now he is referred to as, Richard P. Scaletty P.C.. He had handled many cases for the Scaletty family in the past. Divorces, speeding tickets or he provided advice on small civil cases. Rick was a well-known work comp/ personal injury attorney in Independence, MO. He had built up a medium size law firm just off the square, across from the Jackson County Court House. Just a couple of blocks from Harry Truman's house. He had a big sign out front that read, Law Office. In fact, that's even how they answered the phone at the place. "Law Office!" There were a handful of lawyers that worked out of his building. The firm of McElligott, Ewan & Hall PC. Rick, of course had the largest office down the hall from the reception area. When you entered his office after being summoned, Rick sat in his huge brown leather chair behind an enormous ornate walnut desk. The walls were full of pictures of tropical fish that he had taken on his many vacations' abroad while scuba diving. There were also his lawyer diplomas and the picture and article about him winning his one big case that made him 30 mill. It was a very impressive office to me, his cousin of the same age and just a mere Blue Collar construction worker. But now, I realize that was the point of it all.

Rick lived in a big, fancy house in Lakewood, where many professional athletes and other rich people live, like lawyers. After we talked about and reviewed some of the issues of the case, Rick said that it would be a very strong discrimination case against my employer, and that both a Civil and the Work Compensation case could be handled by his group, and he had just the right guy for the job.

So as my wife, Carrie and I sat in this huge office, Rick assured us that his protégé and good friend, would do us a great service. Rick picked up the desk phone and made a call. "Eric, can you come up to my office, I have some people here I want you to meet." After a few minutes there was a knock at the door. "Come in," said Rick. And in walked a tall, skinny, kind of a geek looking guy about 40. He was wearing a pair of Dockers with no belt and a wrinkled long sleeve shirt without a tie. Rick introduced him, to myself and my wife. "This is my cousin, Mark and his wife, Carrie; Mark and I grew up together. He has a case that I think will be good one for you, Eric." After some small talk, we set up an appointment to return to the 'Law Office' and get going on the case with Eric Roby. And after handshakes from both Rick and Eric, we were out the door and optimistic that justice was finally going to get served.

CHAPTER 2

FOREST LEARNING CENTER/ FLC

I had been working for the Aspen roofing company just a few months. I left my Maintenance Supervisor job with the Kansas City Kansas School District of eight plus years to work for Aspen. I had supervised many out-of-town commercial jobs already and submitted new construction material estimates along with work force requirement bids for many future projects. The company flew me out to Portland, Oregon to look over a new job site that no one from my company had seen yet. Their high-tech aerial view app didn't work high in the mountains evidently. My boss directed me to rent a car at the airport. Drive to Home Depot to buy a 12' Gennie extension ladder. Drive the 100 plus miles north to the job site. Measure that whole roof and roof wings and the various projections of the building, with a tape measure. Then take the ladder back to Home Depot to Returns then drive back to the airport and return home the same night.

This massive building was the Visitors Center for Mt. St. Helens, called The Forest Learning Center. It's located 25 miles from the nearest town of Castle Rock, Washington. We were a sub-contractor for a huge commercial roofing company that had been awarded the contract, but that was to remain a big secret to certain people. I was told not to disclose that fact, or not wear any of my Aspen company clothes with logos. I learned that the State of Washington owned the grounds the building sat on, and Weyerhaeuser owned the building. For some reason my boss did not want the State of Washington or Weyerhaeuser to know who I really worked for. And that's when I started to wonder, what's wrong with this picture and why all the secrecy on such a huge project.

The roof was a typical type of Standing Seam metal roof, dark brown in color. The existing metal roof panels on the main part of the building were the longest at thirty-two feet and two feet wide. All the metal roof panels were to be removed and a new underlayment put down, then new metal roof panels installed. This building design had many different wings and projections with different elevations all around the building. With workers up 35 feet in the air on a 45-degree slope with slick roof conditions and with the probable bad weather coming, I knew this was going to be a job for a dozen skilled journeymen to achieve the outcome my boss wanted.

All the representatives from Weyerhaeuser, Washington State and Centimark met at the site, and we discussed the procedures for safety and protocol for during the roof demo and reconstruction process. They told me to submit daily weather reports, safety checklist, workforce sign in forms and picture documentation submitted daily. And it was made clear that there were NO warnings for any disregard for safety. Any violation of the guidelines and the guilty worker would be expelled from the jobsite indefinitely. I assured them during our meeting that Pat, my boss, would get a knowledgeable crew of skilled workers to meet the two-week demo and installation of the new roof in the timeline that they wanted. Our meeting at the jobsite ended, and I flew back to Kansas City to deliver my proposal and findings to my many bosses. At that meeting were my General Manager, Joe Faunce, the Commercial Manager, Chris Walden and the owner of the company, Pat Nussbeck. I emphasized the concern by the State of Washington and Weyerhaeuser for safety on the work site. I showed them the many pictures I'd taken while on the roof and the many concerns about the two-week timeline with the approaching weather. I also asked why the secrecy issues. That part I didn't understand. But I was assured that I would be given all the resources needed to get the job done and everything would go just fine.

I had been sent to look over leak issues on a newly installed job in Boseman, Montana. There too I was to get with the maintenance man to get access to the roof hatch inside the building. Go up and see what the problems were. Measure for materials that could be sent out to different installers to correct the terrible first install. Take pictures while all the time explaining to the maintenance guy that I was just stopping by to see what a wonderful job they did, and I would be on my way.

So onward with the next project. With the information and measurements from the trip to the Forest Learning Center, I now had to order the new replacement roofing panels at their many different lengths, order what heavy equipment would be required to lift the materials to and from the roof, the various metal trim and flashings for around the windows and doors, safety fencing and barriers to keep the public building open and safe during the construction, a few dumpsters for the recycling and trash and the porta pottys for the workers. Pat told me he was getting the skilled crew together and reserving my motel room and a pickup truck for me to drive while there. I was having serious concerns for this being a smooth-running project. His company had never been a part of such a large metal roof replacement, and he had high hopes of a big profit and a feather in his hat with Centamark. So much so, that Pat didn't even allow his Commercial Manager, Chris to have any input about this particular job. A large commercial metal roofing job such as this would be a huge step for his residential asphalt shingle company. Plus, he had set up his customer with the belief, that with my decades of experience, his company was ready to take on this massive project.

I had done some research, that showed that it rains daily in the fall in Portland, Oregon. The exact time they want this roof to be opened up and exposed to the elements. I felt compelled to mention my weather concerns to Pat. But he scoffed at me and told I wouldn't melt. He said, If it rains all day, it doesn't count against our schedule.

CHAPTER 3

THE HOLLOW LOG

I mentioned that I was Maintenance Foreman for the Kansas City Public Schools for over 8 years. With the 42 buildings that I was responsible for there was an endless list of projects. The Maintenance Department was short staffed. We had been without a director for over a year, there had been no pay increase for the maintenance department for six years, and all the many other issues going on at the District made the offer I received to join Aspen Contracting, very attractive.

Aspen's home office was conveniently located in Lee's Summit, Missouri, and only a mile away from my house.

The General Manager was Larry Hadley and he worked for Aspen for about 6 years. I knew Larry from way back when our sons played Pop Warner football together. My son even dated his daughter while they were in high school. Larry had talked to me numerous times about coming to work for Aspen. He told me that with my commercial roofing knowledge and supervisory experience, I should expect to make at least $150,000.00 my first year as a Project Manager with his company. Larry even told me that I would most likely take over the role as Commercial Manager soon, since the guy they had in place had limited knowledge about metal roofing, and just a little about flat roofs. 'He just had some good contacts' for future work, and Pat used him for that.

So, I pondered my hopes of possibly improving my life with a greater income and I turned in my two weeks' notice at the School District. At 6am the following Monday, I showed up for work at the Aspen Headquarters. I went to the office of Larry Hadley, General Manager. It was first of the week, so his office was crammed full of Mexican Foremen picking up job locations for their crews next residential shingle job. They all left quickly, heading various directions to subdivisions of new construction or to a hail damaged house to tear off and replace shingles. After the commotion ended, Larry handed me an iPad and a list of addresses that he scribbled on a piece of paper. He said, "Go around and sneak up on these guys. Take pictures of them without safety harness or hard hats on and we can fine them and deduct money from their final pay. Ha ha." He had to show me how to turn it on. My first day at Aspen, and I'm part of the management team trying to police their skilled workers taking pictures with my new iPad.

After a few weeks of putting in over 10-hour days chasing the shingle roofers around town, taking their pictures and driving as many as 250 miles in a day, this new job was becoming questionable to say the least. It was not at all like the Commercial Management position Larry promised. He even had me to go up on some of the new roofs and install pipe flashings that the roofers forgot to install. Back to work climbing a ladder, walking roofs with my old tool pouch on. Even cleaning up jobs after the sloppy roofers had left to pick up shingles they threw down onto the ground. Larry told me that most if not all of the workers were illegal immigrants just passing through and the crews personnel change weekly. They were sub-contractors, no insurance, no benefits, no English. They were disposable to him and Aspen it seemed. And both Larry and Pat let the workers know that they could be replaced very easily.

I was noticed by another General Manager that worked at the home office, Joe Faunce. He had talked to me many times about the jobs he had in progress and on the books. He and others noticed how Larry was treating me and wasting my talents. In fact, I had been there months and Larry hadn't even told Pat that he hired me or anything about me. Joe told me that his jobs were more along the commercial line of work I that was hired for. So, Joe got with Pat and had me moved to his office in the same building to be his Project Manager for $500 dollars a week, salary. At the District I was making $1500.00 for 40 hours. I was wondering what had

I done, but remained optimistic. After a couple of weeks, I had supervised many projects that were commercial jobs that Joe's salesman had sold but they didn't have the slightest idea of the roofing method. Many of these new jobs were flat roofs and these salesmen were used to selling shingles for a house. Since I was the only one with the experience with these, I oversaw the jobs while the salesman stood by and watched and hopefully learned something.

It didn't take me long to understand how the company's system was set up either. There was always a big sign out front facing the highway. Salesman Wanted. No Experience will train. The unemployed would venture in right off the street to hear about the many success stories of the salesman. How some made in excess of $100K a year. The company provides you with the training, sales material, business cards, a shirt, and will lend you an iPad for your company transactions. Sounds good! And there's not even a background check. DUI, convict, parole, you can join the team, and you're welcome here. The General Manager will even give you a list of leads to start you on your cold call journey.

All you need to do to be a salesman is to go through the Orientation at the home office for a couple of weeks. You will learn about the company functions of your iPad, learn how to sell a roof to the customer, upsell new windows, gutter and siding. Anything you can get a representative to sign off on that may or may not have been damaged in a storm. They will assign the new salesman to a veteran salesman so they can show you how to set your new ladder you just bought and walk a roof to assess hail damage. Some salesmen had never been up a ladder let alone walk a roof slope. After you have been around that salesman for a week or so, you might be ready to go make some sales on your own. But if you need help on your sale, don't expect to not split your commission with your helper. Your car or truck will need plenty of gas to start down that list of leads you got from your GM. And unfortunately, most of those leads you got, are from past salesman that no longer with the company. But keep positive! You will hear that in your weekly meetings and podcast that you are required to attend. But let's say you got a lead, made an appointment, sold a roof to the homeowner, after you walked it and documented the hail damage you found. You then writeup the proposal and turn in the job at the office. You will be notified when to meet with the Insurance Adjuster later so they can file the claim with the customer. The job will get posted by the Project Manager and there will be lots of scheduling, materials ordered and a crew assigned. Sometimes the various work performed involves different crafts, and more scheduling by the Project Manager is required until the work performed by all crafts is completed, accepted and signed off by the customer. Then when the involved insurance company pays Aspen in full the salesman receives a commission check. This process takes about three months for the new salesman to receive their first commission check. By now however that first check is not there. Most forgot about the many draws they took from their General Manager, just to survive. Of course, your health benefits aren't available until after 90 days, which is typical for employees. But this new hire process is unbearable for most and it's no wonder that not many of the salesman are able to last that long with no income and all the expenses involved. And if they quit, the salesman gives up the jobs that they sold. Those jobs and commission go right back to the General Manager, and any leads go to the next new guy. It was a company of broken promises to me and to other employees I spoke with there. A workplace of unethical work practices, the willful hiring of illegal immigrants, and the different types of discrimination I was subjected to along with other employees. Now when I look back, and after all that has happened and what was discovered, Aspen was just a hollow log of empty promises for me.

CHAPTER 4

OREGON IN OCTOBER

It was a nice sunny day when my plane landed at PDX/ Portland, OR. It was October 6th, 2014. I grabbed my luggage and went over to pick up my rental truck from Hertz. After my insurance was verified, I headed north 50 miles to Kelso, WA. where I would find my motel room waiting. When I arrived at the Motel 6, right off Interstate I-5, there were the usual strolling parking lot hookers and few cars crammed full of what looked like trash but was really peoples' belongings that had been pulled into a few of the parking spaces. It appeared they had been parked there for quite a while. My guess was that they lived here, and they weren't on a vacation stop. I checked into the office where the clerk stood behind a scratched-up bullet proof glass window with a metal slide tray under it. I could tell immediately this wasn't a classy place. My company would always set up my travel arrangements for me, but I always had to pay with my personal credit cards. I was never given a company card. I would turn in my receipts when I would return from my trips, and they would cut me a check for my gas, lodging and other expenses. The clerk found my reservation and said, "If you want Internet its extra. Pay by the week if you like." "Well yeah, I will need that for all my reports." I told him.

I finished in the office and headed upstairs to my home for the next 2 weeks. I made a call back to my office and let my secretary know that the place she reserved for me was "pretty seedy." But I remember her saying something like, …it's only for a couple of weeks, and Pat didn't want to spend too much on your room.

Whatever, I had a 3:30pm meeting I needed to attend at the Forest Learning Center, another 50 miles north up in the mountains. So, worrying about my crappy room wasn't an option right now.

Every day of next week was very busy! I had many meetings to attend with the Weyerhaeuser representative, Steve Meyer and the Centimark representative, Steve Robinwitz. Steve was a nice guy and a good worker. We worked well together that week in getting the job site ready for the crew to arrive anytime. The new roofing materials that I ordered were delivered and staged in the parking lot away from the main building. The chain-link fence I ordered was up and surrounded the material and equipment. Heavy equipment for lifting was fueled up and ready to go.

I had arrived here on Monday and now it was Friday, but still NO CREW had arrived yet. But Pat had been calling me every morning and every evening telling me the crew was on the way, and to just keep stalling them. To make up some excuse to tell them who asked. Then, I got a call at 3:15pm on Friday from Mario, the crew leader. He said that they just arrived and were checking into the motel. I told him I would see them shortly and headed down the mountain to the motel that Aspen had reserved for them. It was a different motel than where they put me.

I used my Garmin GPS to find where the crew was staying. When I arrived at their motel that was on the other side of the small town of Kelso. I was surprised to see that their place more was even more of a shit hole than where I was staying. Management had its perks! There were all kinds of strange looking individuals lingering all over the parking lot. I recognized Mario Meza, a 6' puggy Mexican guy I that was leaning against his parked work truck. I found an empty space and parked my truck. I walked over towards his room where the door was open, and two guys were sitting on the floor inside cooking something in an electric skillet between the two of them. I had known Mario from back in Kansas City from past experiences. Every General Manager, salesmen and even the office people couldn't stand this guy for one reason or another. Mostly his cocky attitude was his biggest fault. My previous experience with his shoddy attempts of workmanship in the past were not pleasant. He must have been self-taught. No wonder Pat was so secretive about who the crew was. Mario shook my hand laughingly and introduced me to his crew. Mario told me, 'You gotta watch that guy,' as he points to one. "He likes to do crack and gets messed up. Sometimes I can't find him for hours. The other guy is afraid of heights but he's a good worker. The two males introduced themselves in Spanish. Not speaking Spanish, I didn't really understand what was said but I did hear the word 'El Salvador', from one.

I went over the safety regulations and Mario interpreted what I said to them. They all signed the form I provided stating they understood all the rules I had just laid out. Then Mario informed me that they didn't bring any Safety equipment with them. Not a Hard Hat, safety vest or harness in the bunch. None of them had any previous experience with this type of roof installation and one of the crew of three feared heights. I was feeling like I was setup and being put into quite a situation. But who was I to tell that to. Now I had to make an unscheduled trip all the way to Portland and buy them all safety gear to work with and be compliant with the rules.

0700! Saturday was a new day. I was optimistic and excited to get the ball rolling! It was 56 degrees and foggy up on the mountain when we arrived. Two members of the new crew were sick, Mario told me. So, they just sat in Mario's truck for hours while I escorted Mario around to survey the job site and for me to point out areas of concern. Around noon it began to mist and light rain started. Mario exclaimed that it's too wet to do any work today. They would just go back to the motel. About then the passenger side door on Mario's truck opens and one of his workers walks from the truck and walks over by the cliff. He crawls over the 4-foot barrier that keeps the public away from the cliff edge that is more than 200-foot drop straight down to the valley below created by the volcano. The guy stands at the edge of the cliff while singing in Spanish and taking a video of himself doing so. Mario is laughing while I am yelling at the guy to get back! He slowly finished his video and strolled back to the truck and got in. They drive away slowly, and the crew headed back to their motel. I made another one of my many calls back to Pat to report how the day one went.

Sunday. Workday two. Rain started again at 1:45pm and another unproductive workday. Mario told me that Pat called him last night and told him he only must listen to Pat, not to me. I know Pat is talking behind my back with Mario. That's what Pat does, and he's also having conversations with the Centimark rep. while also keeping any truths from the Weyerhaeuser guy. I was having a hard time keeping all of Pats lies straight. And not being included in any of these conversations made me feel even more puzzled and betrayed than ever.

Monday, Monday, Mario and his helper are up on the roof, they removed one of the panels and start to slide it down the 45% slope of the roof, I can see they have no rope attached to the long piece of metal in case they were to lose their grasp. This was an accident ready to happen. Down on the ground stands the shortest of the Mexican workers. The one that said he feared heights, so he is the ground man. Mario's plan was for this ground guy to reach up and catch this two-foot wide by thirty-two feet long and approximately 200-pound panel. They would slide it down the roof slope, and then he could lay it on the ground after it drops off the roof edge. I was witnessing what was going on and was about to happen. I yelled up to Mario to hold the panel. But he continued to slide the panel down the slope. The bottom end of the panel is over the roof edge but is still too high in the air for the short guy to reach up and grab. I can see the catastrophe that's about to happen and realize there's no way this one man can possibly be expected to catch and land this. I hurried over to assist before the guy gets crushed and I reached up and grabbed the panel since I was taller. He finally grabbed hold of the panel behind me about when it fell off the edge of the roof. The panels weight and length were too much for even both of us to manage and of course and it crashed to the ground as we both let go of it. I felt a sharp pain in my left shoulder immediately, and I was mad that these clowns were so reckless in their work method. I told Mario and his crew that they would find a different way to remove those panels from now on. I reported my injury to Pat that afternoon during another one of our many talks, but he was more concerned about getting the job done than my hurting shoulder. He was mad I even helped trying to land the panel. I could tell the problems were just beginning with this crew selection.

Forget about the two-week completion date! Over the next three weeks we worked every day in the rain or shine. There were countless safety violations that I documented in my reports and sent to Pat. As well as the unsuccessful attempts at production that I included in my daily reports. My pictures and reports were so incriminatingly explicit that my office shut my iPad off. I guess they felt that prevented me from documenting what was going on, meant that it wasn't going on. I started using my phone to take pictures of safety violations and would text Pat the pictures. I didn't want him to miss out on what was happening. I was keeping him very well aware of the reality of the fiasco, and that really made him mad. I knew the truth of what was really going on would certainly damage the façade he created about his company to Centimark. Pat was telling the customer that everything was fine at the job site.

Mario's pathetic attempts were looking bad for Pat. So, he contacted and hired a five-man Aspen roofing crew from Portland to come up and help out. But after a few days of working with Mario, they left and returned to Portland. Stating that Pat had lied to them about the pay they were to receive, plus they didn't like working with Mario for several reasons. Mario's mouth and attitude. He was even condescending to the workers that were there to help. I asked Pat for permission to hire a half dozen temp workers from Portland. I was desperate to make some progress. This job was becoming a laughingstock with these clowns. But Pat nor I were laughing. Even the temp workers quit after a week, due to the unsafe practices of Mario and his crew. I hired five more workers from the temp service. The count was getting high of the near misses I had documented where Mario's workers would drop and send heavy rolls of roofing underlayment or heavy pry bars sliding down the roof slope towards other workers. They nearly knocked some temp workers off the roof on a couple of occasions. The temp workers came to me to complain about Mario and his crew. I asked for them to write statements and sign them which I included in my Daily Report. They all stated that Mario had made it a very unsafe work environment and he refused to take orders or direction from me. But Pat didn't seem to care about any of that. He didn't really like Mario but protected him. Mario was all he had for traveling installer, and Mario knew it. I tried to contact my Commercial Manager, Chris Walden, to keep him involved about all the issues I was having, but he wouldn't even return my phone calls or emails even though he was the Centimark contact for Aspen. Pat had full control of this one.

There was week after week of various issues, including the new installed panels blowing off because of high winds. Mario was not fastening them properly for this application and leaks were appearing inside the building. Water was running down the walls inside and about to do serious damage to the pricey artifacts of the museum.

Pat decided that he should send another 'manager' out from KC to get this job done. It had now been a month since the had job started and it was not even a fourth completed yet. I welcomed any help and anyone that thought they could get production from this bunch of knuckleheads.

On October 29th, Pat Casey, a salesman they were trying to promote to a manager showed up at the jobsite. I handed over all the keys I had for the equipment, gates and such. Pat told me to head over to a job in Gresham, OR. where some roofers had finished. He directed me to clean up the mess they made and to load up and the unused bundles of shingles in my truck and return to the supplier for credit. Those dozen muddy bundles were about 60 pounds each. My injured shoulder felt every pound. Then I was to check out of my Motel 6 and meet Kevin Treece at the Portland airport at 7:30pm tomorrow. Pat said, 'give him your keys to your truck and he will take you to your new motel closer to the airport where you will fly back tomorrow morning.' I drove down to the airport to meet Kevin at his gate.

We exchanged greetings and handshakes, and I told him let's head over to the Hertz desk, we can get this truck insurance information transferred over in your name. But Kevin said, "No wait, I don't have a license, it was taken away years ago, drugs and DUI's. Pat knows that." What! I immediately made a call to Pat. I said to him, "What the hell, you send some guy out here with NO license to drive a truck that's in my name!?"

Immediately, Pat started screaming obscenities at me told me let him take the truck. I hung up on him and drove myself and Kevin to my new motel. I gave him the keys and said, "If that truck is still in my name tomorrow, I will call the police and report it stolen."

I flew back to Kansas City where my wife, Carrie picked me up. We talked on the drive home about the month-long fiasco, and she couldn't believe it. The next morning was Saturday, I got up and headed directly to the Quick Care that was close to my house. With all the commotion going in Washington State, I was not allotted any time nor permitted to tend to medical attention while there. My shoulder injury weeks before had been long forgotten about by everyone. The incomplete job in Washington was the elephant in the room. But the intense pain was with me nonstop from the time it happened. Dr. Johnson was on staff at the Quick Care that morning. He looked and felt my shoulder, but no Xray was taken. He gave me prescription for pain medicine and a light duty form to give my employer. I was to do no lifting, no reaching, no climbing and no lifting over 5-pounds with no driving or operating heavy equipment while taking the narcotic drugs.

Mario has a disregard for orders from Mark (supervisor). He expresses that he doesn't care about things like wearing a harness or safty vest. Its like he doesn't care.

Eric Rivera (ASAP)

Eric Rivera 360-423-0036

On 10/22/14 at St Helens Job site there was disregaurd to all safty rules by marios crew/ tools falling off Roof/ Being told to put Safty Rop/ hard hats on/ being told more then once by supervisor (Mark).

Lonney Roller

L Roller (ASAP)

423 0036

On 10/27/14 at a roofing Job they were just trowing staff off the Roof carelessly and Mario was told many time they when he seen the ware houser guy he huirred up and put the Roop/ hard hat on.

Matthew orr ASAP

360-423-0036

CHAPTER 5

BACK HOME

When I walked into my office on Monday morning, I noticed how many things had changed. My pictures that I had on my office wall of various projects I had worked on had been removed. At my desk sat my General Manager, Joe Faunce. He told me he liked my office better, so he took it over. Maybe because I had all the production boards on my wall, it did make it easier for him to see. I looked over into his office next door to see his desk was cleared, and the lights were off. There were two other salesmen standing in the room with Joe when I entered, but neither one of them spoke to me. It was like I was invisible. In fact, ever since I had entered the building, no one had spoken or even recognized me to say hello. Not a single welcome back, how was your trip. Strange. Then, my cell phone rang, it was Pat. I went out into the hallway to take the call. "Give all your keys and your iPad to Larry Hadley and leave the building. I will give you further instructions." I walked down and found Larry in his office. It seemed like he was waiting for me. This was clearly a prearranged setup. I did as Pat instructed and left the building and got into my personal truck and went home.

Almost a week went by and there was no communication from the office. Then on Friday, I received a text on my phone from Pat. It said, "Be in the conference room on Monday morning at 8am." Monday came, and I was there slightly before and ushered into the conference room by a receptionist. I sat in there alone for over 15 minutes. Remembering the sales meetings, we had in here. Many of the managers would sit around the huge table with the high back racecar looking seats with the company logo on them. We would have conference calls with other managers from around the country. Pat loved to brow beat and humiliate them while they were on the call. He would cuss them out and then snicker quietly at us while they were apologizing to him. Pat loved the public display of ridicule against his employees. I expect his five-foot four-inch stature might have something to do with this behavior. But maybe that's how millionaires act, I'll never know.

Then into the conference room came Pat and Susan Swisher. She was the Office Manager. They took seats across the table from me. It appeared like I was set up for a trial. Pat started out blaming me for all the problems and issues that took place on the job in Washington. It was my own fault I got hurt, my fault that Mario had so many issues, and even my fault it rained so much. Pat suggested that I should quit right now. He even told me that no one here likes you.

Wow! I was shocked. I had gone from Employee of the Month to mud in just two short months? I told him that quitting was not an option for me. That with my son competing as an athlete in college, I needed to keep him insured for him to be eligible. But Pat's animosity towards me was because I challenged him about the truck incident. He didn't like anyone that would dare talk back. He was a millionaire that owned a roofing company but had never installed a roof. He made millions off the insurance racket wind and hail damage gig. You know, taking advantage of people when they literally don't have a roof over their head. Pat only wanted yes men around him. And because of what I did, I would now be reduced to a Commission only Roofing Salesman. That entry level starting position I talked about earlier. And try selling roofs at the end of the year in November when it's snowing in Kansas City. One might find it to be difficult. My management position that was promised by Hadley, was over. Pat told me he had plenty more jobs back in Kansas City that I would supervise when I returned but that was another lie. The doctor put me on "Light Duty" and Pat knew my restrictions. The prescription meds they prescribed prohibited me from driving, let alone climbing ladders onto roofs. He knew that I was going to Physical Therapy three times a week for hours each day. He was just setting me up, and I knew it.

Pat said since I was going to continue to work for Aspen, I should get with Joey Trotta. He was the son of Laura Trotta the IT specialist with the company. Joey was to give me the orientation that I never received as a new hire. Joey retrieved my iPad back and handed it back to me. I turned it on and realized that everything had been completely erased. All my pictures, contacts, emails and any thing I had on it was gone. Of course, Joey didn't know anything about that. His mom would be the one that would do that at Pats direction. His job was just to give me the company orientation and go over company policy and procedure, since I had apparently skipped training thanks to Larry. After a few days of training with Joey, I was ready to go out and be an entry level commission only salesman. Welcome back.

With all the restrictions from the doctor and the pain medicine they had me on, restricted my driving. I sure couldn't climb ladders to get onto roofs to look at perspective jobs or take measurements that would be required to bid jobs. I did my best by preparing bids by going to OfficeMax and printing off large blueprints from the internet and estimating jobs with the resources I had, a ruler and calculator on my dining room table. But getting the vital pricing information and material cost from anyone at Aspen was fruitless. I wasn't even invited to the weekly conference calls anymore. I was being avoided and the managers would take forever to answer my calls or emails if they did at all. I researched some new software by GradeBeam that would make estimating for myself and others so much easier and more proficient. I set up a demo of the software, but Pat declined it because it cost 2000 bucks. Even though it would save the estimators countless hours of time bidding jobs in the future with much more proficiency. Pat blocked my every effort to bid new work and I believe he put the word out to other managers to not provide me pricing information that I would need to complete or submit bids on time. He was more interested in punishing me and making an example for others to see what happens to employees that dare to call him out on his behavior.

Then after six months of painful rehab of stretching a few times a week, that did nothing to heal my aching shoulder, I had no sales to turn in and no new work on the books. I had made absolutely no income of any kind for over six months even after working from home for somedays for ten hours doing estimating. They turned off my iPad once again and Pat sent me an email telling me I was fired for failure to do my job. He accomplished his task, to get rid of me.

Now it's important to know that after I came home to Kansas City from Washington, I'd made a call to my cousin Rick and explained my situation and what happened out there. It was during that first week back that I met with Eric Roby at the Law Office. Roby and I were in constant contact during those 6 months before I was fired and doing the best I could to just survive and keep providing for my son. After the first of the year, Roby had the case moved from Washington to Missouri, since Aspen was based there. Eric and Rick were emailed often about situations I was experiencing at work so they would know what I was going through. Roby told me he was going to file multiple suits, that being the Workman's Comp and the civil suit. I told Roby often how I was struggling to get any jobs, and how I physically just couldn't do it. But Roby never gave me advice on how to proceed at work. Never advised me what to say or not to say to people, or things to do or not do. Just hang in there stuff. "Everything was going to be alright. We're gonna' get em'."

CHAPTER 6

DOCTOR, DOCTOR

Even after I was fired, I was still going to Physical Therapy three times a week until May. I know my body and I knew that this stretching crap wasn't improving anything but my pain level. I guess I was in a bad mood that day I went in and demanded that I have an MRI. They took my advice and scheduled it for a week later at Centerpoint Hospital in Independence, Missouri. I got the results back within a couple of days and they saw four large tears in my rotator cuff and my bicep tendon was torn off. This was going to require some Orthoscopic surgery on top of my shoulder and under my armpit. No wonder those fifty-pound bundles of shingles that Pat had me load up and return before I flew back to Kansas City felt so heavy. Surgery was scheduled for July 22. I had gone nine months of terrible pain after my injury in Washington, before real measures to help were even scheduled.

In the meantime, Carrie and I had gotten married. We had been together since I worked for the school district. She knew of my recent issues at Aspen, we talked every day while I was working in Washington. I blind copied the emails and pictures that I included in my reports to her. I knew early on with this company to cover my ass with these clowns. We flew to Jamaica for a wonderful and beautiful wedding and honeymoon. We both sold our houses an bought a beautiful 4000 square foot brick ranch style house in Lees Summit, Missouri. An upscale suburb in eastern Jackson County. This was going to be our dream home, together, forever.

I was ready to finally get my shoulder fixed. I had been anxiously waiting for this day. My surgeon was Dr. Aakash Shaw. I met him as I was being prepped for my outpatient procedure that he said would take a little over an hour. He foresaw no problem with the surgery. He was very reassuring to myself, Carrie and my son Matt that had accompanied us for my outpatient surgery. They were ushered to the waiting room while the nurses got me wired up and the IV going. I asked when they were going to shave me, and they said when you're asleep. Ha ha. They gave me some pills to swallow and kept adding something to the IV. The doctor came in and looked at the monitor a few times. Then another doctor came in and looked at it but didn't say anything. I had been laying here prepped for an hour and I hadn't moved from the pre op area. Something was obviously wrong, and I knew it.

Finally, the doctor came back, along with my wife and son. Doctor Shaw said, "Well I've got some good news for you and some bad news". Hmmmm OK? So, tell me the good news, I said. "Well, the good news is that you're not going to get operated on today. The bad news is your heart rate is still at 136 and that's even with the medications we have given you. You are about to have a stroke. We have notified the ER next door at the hospital, and they are waiting for you now".

My wife looked on horror, my son was on the verge of tears. I didn't know what the hell was going on. I got myself dressed and we walked hand in hand in kind of a daze the short walk over to the ER at Menorah Hospital.

Boy the doctor was right, they were ready. They put me on a table and were like a NASCAR pit crew. They inserted an IV in each arm and wired me up like a robot. There must have been four nurses running around that ER room doing stuff. Carrie and Matt sat silently seated against the wall watching the camotion. The nurse handed me a pill and a cup of water. I made a joke that I would rather have a Coors light to wash it down with. I guess my humor wasn't felt in the ER like I intended, because no one laughed. That nurse came back over towards me, grabbed a chair, sat down, and got her face right in my face. She said, "You don't seem to take this seriously, do you? Don't you realize what could happen to you if we don't get this taken care of. You are on the verge of a stroke!" I swallowed hard.

The next couple hours in the ER were solemn ones. I realized I wasn't invincible anymore. They finally got my heart rate down and I was released. The hospital assigned a Cardiologist named Doctor Stephen Bloom. He was an easy-going guy that wore blue jeans every visit I remember. I was diagnosed with having Atrial Flutter. A condition in which the hearts upper chambers beat too quickly. I was on Eliquis, beata blockers, pain meds and with no shoulder operation in site until all the heart issues got taken care of. I was given a heart monitor to wear 24 hours a day. It hung around my neck with three wires that were attached on me with sticky pads and had to be changed daily.

Doctor Bloom performed a Cardioversion on me on September 1st. The shock thing that leaves burn marks on your chest and back. I would now be on medications and wearing the heart monitor for 24 hours a day for the next three months. The doctor could see my heart rate being transmitted to a source in his office and make medication adjustments at our bi-weekly visits. After a week, I just shaved my whole chest. Tearing those pads off daily or before a shower hurt! And you must relocate them around on your chest but stay in the same area for them to work properly. It sucked. Finally, I was stable enough to get rid of the heart monitor and get off the medications. My stress level had gone way down. I know that Carrie had a calming effect on me, and that's what helped. The cariologist stated that my heart issues were most likely caused from all the pain and stress from the injury. Plus, all the added stress from loss of income, loss of job and career, selling a house buying a house, the bills and copays from treatments was very overwhelming. I was lucky to have Carrie, she was the only stable thing I had now in my life. This heart problem was a big thing. I was unaware of any history of heart problems in my family, but it was time to really investigate. My findings would answer many of the questions I'd had all my life and would change me forever.

CHAPTER 7

LONG LOST FAMILY

This new heart problem was not what I needed in addition to all the other legal issues I had. I was 62 years old, in in pretty good condition health wise except for the torn rotator cuffs in each shoulder. My right shoulder had been operated on in 2005 from another work comp injury and I ended up with 21% total permanent disability in that shoulder. My yearly physicals were always good with no weight or cholesterol issues, and I only took a one-a-day silver vitamin as any medication, up until now. I had never done genealogy research before; I really wasn't interested in it. But now, for medical reasons I felt I needed to know some heart history.

I was born in Kansas City, Missouri on June 27th in 1953 in the old St. Vincent's Hospital. My mother, named me Matthew. It was changed to Mark a few months later when I was adopted by John and Virginia Scaletty. They were the best parents I could have ever been blessed with. They provided me with a 12-year Catholic school education at private schools and were both pillars in the community. My father passed in 2008, but I was taking care of my mother at the time and thought she might have some medical information about me. I knew I needed to ask her.

I was somewhat hesitant to talk to my mom about possibly doing a parent search, but I asked her if she knew anything when I went to see her that day. I had never seen my original birth certificate or any documentation that they might have from the adoption process. I remember being told by my parents that I was adopted at a very young age. It wasn't a secret in our family. She understood my concerns completely to find out medical information, but she had no information other than my given name was Matthew Dart.

I contacted the Missouri Department of Social Services in a letter indicating my desire for contact with my biological parents. Missouri law at the time, required that both the adoptee and the biological parent must voluntarily register prior to them providing identifying information. But they had nothing for me.

I received a letter from the Circuit Court of Missouri. They told me how the law allowed the adopted adult to hire a search agency to contact the birth parents and determine if they are willing to give out their identity. So, I hired what was called a Search Angel. Her name was Laura Long. She asked lots of questions and got lots of information from me and told me she would get back when she found out anything. She called a few days later to let me know that both of my parents had passed a few years previous. I was sad about that, I guessed I should have done this years ago. Dang! But then Laura's tone changed. She asked me, "would you be interested in meeting any of your siblings?" Wow! My mind had been so focused on retrieving medical news from my parents that I hadn't even thought about siblings. I said sure why not.

Laura told me to write a letter to my relations telling them a little bit about myself and what I expected from this. I wrote the letter, saying that I was married with four children, 13 grandchildren, my hobbies and my address, phone number and email address. I wasn't hiding anything; this was getting interesting. I faxed the letter I had prepared over to Laura. She said that she would also write a letter letting the recipients know that this wasn't a scam and she added her contact information if they wanted to go through her instead of me. I didn't really know what I expected to happen next.

I was sitting in the bleachers on a Saturday a week later watching my son in a track meet out of town. My phone rang, and a strange number I didn't recognize appeared on the caller I.D.. I got up and left the bleachers to take the call around behind them to get away from all the noise of the crowd, but it was too late, they had hung up. Since sometimes my mom's assisted living place would call if there was a problem, I immediately called the number back. A female voice answered and said, "Hello?" I replied, "Hello, this is Mark." The female said, "I hear you're my, brother?" I replied, "That's what I've been told."

That was the very first contact that I had with my younger sister, Carla. And that was the first contact I had ever experienced with a blood relation. There would be many more calls and visits to come from my long-lost family. Some secrets about our family would be revealed soon.

Many of the questions people had remained a mystery for over 50 years would be answered. Since then, I have been able to meet with almost all my 16 siblings.

My father, Clinton Johnson and mother, Marcene Dart with their multiple marriages and hanky panky had produced eight children on my mother's side and eight on my father's side. Some of my brothers and sisters have passed even since our first meeting, and I have visited their graves. Carrie and I hosted a wonderful reunion at our house where my brothers and sisters that had never met or even knew of each other were united. My birth mother had left three of her sons with their fathers upon divorce and never saw the boys again. The younger children were never told about their older siblings. My father was separated from his wife when he made me. I was a big secret in that house. Then he left town with his family when he found out my mom was pregnant. My brother on that side made the comment at the reunion, "So that's why we had to move to California, it was because of you!"

I guess I was the secret. My mom was poor and in-between marriages, and she sure couldn't take care of me. I am glad she chose adoption and not the alternative. I have stayed in touch with all my many new family members. Every one of them have been loving and welcoming to myself and my family. My mom, Virginia, loved seeing the pictures of us and how many similarities there are in our facial features. She wanted to meet them, but Covid screwed that up and she passed at 98 years old in 2021.

I have found out so much more information since then. First, there was no history with either family of heart problems. That was the main thing I was searching for. But second, I did a 23andMe genealogy search and found out some astonishing information and history about my birth family history.

Through the in-depth research with other new family members, we have traced back to relationship to three families that were on the Mayflower. I discovered I am Norwegian, Swedish and English. A descendent of many kings and descendent from several signers of the Declaration of Independence. Related to signer, Benjamin Harrison V. Son, William Henry Harrison, 9th President and great grandson, Benjamin Harrison 23rd President of the United States. Yes, also cousins of the Pawn Star guys.

A not-so-distant cousin is the current Prime Minister of United Kingdom, Boris Johnson. And Edwin Powell Hubble. He built a telescope. My 7th cousin Gilbert Clifford Noble of Barnes and Noble. Marjorie Merriweather Post of Post cereal, the Wright brothers, Anthony Perkins of Psycho, Elizabeth Montgomery, William Scott 'Jack" Elam, John Cena and a writer by the name of JRR Tolkien. The way it's been going I'm sure there will be more distant cousins that genealogy will produce.

It is a blood relation that I had never had before. New brothers and sisters, cousins, nephews and nieces. A new family in support of me and my efforts to find justice. I even found out my new brothers in laws brother was married to the judge hearing my work comp case. It's a small world. And it's closing in.

CHAPTER 8

MOTIONS AND EMOTIONS

I was very relieved that the information I had received from interviewing my long-lost family that there was no history of heart problems in the family. This confirmed my belief that all the stress from Roby and the Aspen case was working as they planned. They just wanted me gone. Especially now I knew too much about their operation, I got injured and was going to cost them money.

I had many cardiologist appointments in the next few months. Fortunately, Carrie and I had gotten married right before this happened. Aspen had cancelled my health insurance before I was fired, and I hadn't received any offer for COBRA or an alternative. We had no idea until the ER refused my Aspen insurance card. Every ER expense, testing, doctor visits, medication and co pay was either out of pocket or Carrie's Blue Cross Blue Shield had to cover it. Thousands of dollars in expenses were adding up, and it was all on us.

Eric Roby, my young attorney said he had everything under control, however. Keep track of those receipts, he kept saying. I was fired in April of 2014, and it wasn't until July of 2016, when Roby said he filed 23 orders, motions, interrogatories', certificate of service, he got the jury trial scheduled along with hearings. Maybe these two cases were finally going to get resolved.

Roby had scheduled me to go see a particular doctor he said Rick used often for ratings. He would give us the numbers that we wanted. He set up the visit with Dr. Stuckmeyer, in downtown Lee's Summit. The doctor had quite a peculiar office, I thought. It was in one of the hundred-year-old brick buildings on the square. There was nothing that indicated it was a doctor's office from the outside or looking in the window. The room looked to be full of antiques and had a huge fish aquarium against one wall. It looked more like an antique store, really. There was a desk for a receptionist to sit, but it was empty and cleared off. The doctor welcomed me in, and we walked into his office through a doorway from the main area. The doctor looked to be in his 80's and was dressed like a Charles Dickens character and had big bushy eyebrows. He asked me some questions about my cousin, Rick and how he was doing. He never mentioned Roby. Then he told me to stand up and hold out my arms like a cross. He sat behind his desk and said, "Oh yes, I can see you have trouble there". I put my arms down and that was the end of his exam. The doctor said he would prepare a statement and get it over to Rick's office. My visit probably lasted a whole 12 minutes if that. I left, went home and sent an email to Roby telling him the exam was completed.

In January of 2017, we had our first court date for the Work Comp case on the 13th. I was so excited to finally get something underway. Roby informed me a week later that it had been cancelled, saying the judge was out sick. In April, Roby and I had a few meetings scheduled to practice for my deposition for the third of May coming up. Roby cancelled those three meetings the morning of the meetings and rescheduled for the day before the deposition. Roby told me they would probably just ask some dumb questions and we would be done before noon. For preparation for my upcoming deposition, he put me in a small room with a tv and had me watch a VHS video about how to take a deposition. That was all he had me do for preparation. My guess was, he felt ready for tomorrow.

I had never been in a deposition before. I grew anxious as the stenographer arrived and set up his equipment. Eric was bouncing around from the upstairs office and back down to the conference room which was in the dingy basement at the law office. I believe he was anxiously waiting for the Aspen lawyer, J. Daniel Weidner, who was a hired gun out of Omaha that delt in Construction Litigation. Roby figured Nussbeck, his boss and client would be there for intimidation purposes. It was evident that Roby was nervous about the whole thing.

At 8:20am, a man around 45 years old, in a pinstriped suit with a pressed white shirt, tie and cuff links walked in. He carried a stack of papers, binders and folders over a foot tall. He entered the conference room and set his paperwork on the opposite side of the table of where I was seated. He introduced himself as, Daniel Weidner. Pat wasn't with him however, I figured he would be for intimidation purposes. That was Pat's style, but I found out quickly this guy wouldn't need any help in that department. Weidner looked around the conference room and at the enormous collection of law books on the shelves at each end of the room from floor to ceiling. "You still use these? They have everything online now, Eric. Maybe you guys need to get up to speed". His condescending attitude right off the bat made me cringe. I asked him, "What time do you think we will get finished today? I need to take my mom to the doctor later this afternoon."

"You won't be seeing mom today. We have a lot to go over. You will be lucky to get out of here before dark." He said laughingly.

Sure enough, the deposition for that day was over at 7:00pm. That evening. Roby, my lawyer, sat quietly through the whole thing as I was blamed for everything that had gone wrong in the last six months. Roby only Interrupted or objected a couple of times in those grueling hours of questioning. I felt totally alone and I was frustrated in the way I was being asked the same question five different ways by this cocky S.O.B.. I finally said, "Look, I'm just an injured worker trying to receive a fair compensation for my injury." Weidner just smirked and chuckled silently. I asked him, "Do you think this is funny." He scolded back, "Mr. Scaletty, I love God, my country, my wife and my family. I am a very happy man. I'm sorry if my smile offends you so much!"

There was just a few more hours of questioning that evening. We resumed the deposition a week later. This time the questioning was for only six hours. Again, there was never an interruption from Roby about anything. Just his usual asking to go to the restroom about every hour or so. I guess he needed to powder his nose.

Eric Roby and I met a few more times in the next couple of months. He cancelled more meetings at the last minute even after I had driven across town and was at his office waiting for him to show up. He would call and say, sorry, can't make it. Wife was sick, kids were sick, he was sick. What I didn't know was that while all this was happening; petitions were being filed, there were motions for sanctions, affidavits filed, hearings scheduled, case management, dismissals, jury trial scheduled. But Roby wasn't following up on anything, and his office was allowing this to happen. They had no more idea what this jack wagon was doing any more than he did. It would be years until we knew the truth of what was really happening at the law office.

Roby told me we had our work comp trial coming up in July. He scheduled a few meetings with Carrie and I to go over the many issues about this case. Since I had a previous work-related injury, this new disability would make me eligible for what is called The Second Injury Fund, in Missouri. It provides additional compensation to workers that have a percentage of disability that I would be eligible for.

But wouldn't you know it, that judge got sick and cancelled. Our court case was postponed again. Carrie had made plans to visit her daughter in NC and had postponed her trip for this? She was furious with Eric and let him know about it. This was one of many dates that Roby said we had to be available for things and couldn't plan very much. No leaving the city or travels. We had to stay close in case he needed us for something.

Roby assured us that he was really going to pile on the offenses for all they had done. First, they got me hurt. Then fired me and offered no insurance options. Then all the thousands of dollars that we had to pay out of pocket for the heart issues they caused. He was even going to get them for my heart problems that were certainly caused by them maliciously.

Roby was pilling up the offenses and making sure we knew that I was going to be sitting pretty when we collected all the money, I had coming from the work comp case and the civil suit. Roby exclaimed that he was giddy with excitement about how easy this case was to prove against them.

The way things were going even Roby said he was surprised at how screwed up the court system was. Judges getting sick all the time and cancelling. And he just didn't understand how everything took so long. He said it was all Aspens fault. They were purposely dragging their feet at every step of the process making it difficult for him and me. He said they were really out to get me. They were trying to starve me out, so to speak, and if they continued to be assholes much longer, he suggested that I take matters into my own hands. He suggested that I should go after them physically. This whole thing was becoming a complete nightmare, hard for anyone to understand and even Roby said, "This is such a wild story no one would ever believe it. Maybe you should write a book."

CHAPTER 9

LIAR LIAR

With the Work Comp case cancelled in January, it wasn't until July 27th that Roby was able to get it rescheduled. But just our luck, it was cancelled again because this judge got sick just like the other one before.

Then in March of 2019, Roby scheduled three meetings in preparation for our new court date in April. However, Roby cancelled two of those meetings and three other scheduled meetings in April because of issues he said he had at home. Any meetings that Carrie attended were always in Ricks office. Roby loved to sit behind his hero's large desk and play lawyer. I guess because he didn't have an office for himself. If we weren't in Rick's office, then we would meet in the conference room in the basement.

Finally, on April 24th we were finally ready go to Work Comp court. That appearance was cancelled alike the previous. But Roby reassured me that with the depositions he had lined up for May 9th and 10th, Nussbeck and his office staff, were going to be squirming. It was his turn to ask the questions now. He was ready this time and said was furious at how the court system and Aspen was treating me.

I was at the law office early the day of the depositions. I was glad to be sitting on the other side of the table. Roby had me write down a list of questions that I thought he should ask them. I was excited that my lawyer would be putting the heat on with his pointed questions he said he had prepared. I wanted to hear them answer to why he told the employees not to talk to me. Why would managers not answer my phone calls or emails for pricing. Why he had I.T. turn off my iPad. Their answers would prove retaliation.

I awaited in the basement conference room. Roby came in and said that he had seen the court stenographer just pull in the parking lot out front. Alright, show time! A half hour passed but yet no one came into the conference room. I sat there alone waiting. Then Roby came in and said that Nussbeck had called with some kind of issue that he had to attend to, and he wouldn't be there for the deposition today. Roby told me that it was a good thing he caught that stenographer outside before she had set up or he would have had to pay her.

There was never a stenographer scheduled and Nussbeck was never dispositioned. Lies!

Roby said he would reschedule with them. And all the time that they were wasting of his was being added onto their bill. He reassured me that they were not going to get away with this type of contempt.

July 3rd was a beautiful Saturday afternoon. I had just returned home from a motorcycle ride where I viewed the Vietnam Traveling Wall, with some friends. I sat down in my recliner to tell my wife about the experience, when Carrie exclaimed, "I'm done! I can't do this anymore. The moving truck will be here Tuesday." I couldn't say I blamed her for leaving. She didn't deserve what she was being put through with my work injury, my lawyer or the court shenanigans. She knew I was in constant pain from my shoulder injury. She witnessed my attitude change because of the way things were going the last five years with these two never-ending cases. Roby had insisted numerous times that we had to remain in the city for various meetings with him and for the depositions he kept scheduling and then cancelling. Don't plan anything, stay close to Kansas City in case I need you for something, he would say. And do not do any activity outside the house or anywhere that their insurance investigator could find damaging to the case. Nothing physical that may draw attention. Roby assured me that with the money that Aspen had, they had people watching me. He had many more suggestions, now that my wife left me, and I had nothing. I told him all this tension was too much for my marriage. They damn near killed me with the heart issue caused by the stress. And now since my wife had left me because of this case, he was going to add my marriage failure to the huge list of other offenses he conjured up. It was like he had a menu of violations with their value on it. He said my marriage was worth another hundred thousand dollars.

Now I was stuck with out an income and left with a 4000 square foot house to sell. I didn't see a bright ending to this nightmare anytime soon.

I put our beautiful brick ranch style house on the market. I hired a Real Estate Agent that was a daughter of a friend. Of course, I couldn't ever catch a break with that deal. She took advantage of me and sold it to the first couple that walked in the door just so she could make a quick buck and be on her way. I had a few high-end appliances; washer, dryer and a stainless-steel side by side refrigerator that she knew I couldn't take in my move. She wanted them for her son's house. So, she low balled me and got what she wanted. I was desperate for any cash and she saw an easy target.

I finally had some money to survive on for a bit. I also had to sell much of my musical instruments, amplifiers, speakers and other equipment to get a little more cash. Then I moved in with a friend in Kansas City. I really had nowhere else to go.

In late July, Roby and I had a meeting with the judge at the Missouri Division of Employment Security.

I met Roby at the law office, and we rode together in his car. What a piece of crap car my lawyer had. I think it was an older Ford Escort or something, dirty on the outside and inside. With trash and candy wrappers on the floor and little kids' stuff scattered in the back seat. We drove to the large building that's located in the Kansas City, Missouri bottoms near where the old stockyards exchange used to be. We walked inside the modern looking two-story building and went up an escalator then down a hallway. There were small conference rooms on one side of the hall with glass windows. Roby led me into one and told me to have a seat, then said we were a little early and we could just wait in here until the judge was ready to see us.

After a couple of minutes, Roby got up and said he had to go to the restroom and left the room. He returned about 20 minutes later and seemed overjoyed. He said he just had a meeting with the judge. While going to the restroom the judge had seen him in the hallway and so they had a conversation and had gotten everything taken care of. We were all done here! This seemed almost too easy. I had prepared and I was wanting my time with the judge. But Roby assured me things were going just fine.

In August we had another meeting scheduled with the Second Injury Fund judge that would sign off on the additional compensation that I would be receiving. That meeting was cancelled and rescheduled for September. This was the meeting I was awaiting. The judge was my brothers, brother's wife. Not related, but I felt that I would finally get a fair shake given all that had happened. I had written a heartfelt letter to Judge Emily Fowler. Telling her about my years of issues with the representation I was receiving, my concerns about the court system with all its cancellations and how this whole case had affected my life and health and my marriage. Roby reviewed my letter and said that it would be entered as evidence in my case.

Roby told me that Judge Fowlers court was in the Jackson County Court House in Independence, Missouri. Since the law office was located just across the street, we walked to the courthouse from the law office. We were screened at the security check points just inside the door. I was excited to see the judge today. We had met once before at my brother's funeral, and she seemed compassionate enough in our conversation, that I felt her to be someone I could finally trust in the judicial system.

Roby found a conference room for us to go into to wait until Judge Fowler would see us. He told me to have a seat and excused himself for another rest room visit. He returned in about ten minutes. Again, mysteriously he said had met with the judge in the hallway. He told he gave her my letter that I had written to her and that she would enter it into the case file. We were done with another court appearance. Roby made court so easy, but I was becoming suspicious, of him and the whole process.

Our civil case court date was coming up quickly. There was a hearing scheduled with Judge Cain for September 25th. But Roby had not been able to get the people from Aspen in the office for depositions yet due to everyone's conflicting schedules. Roby cancelled the hearing with the judge because of that reason and scheduled for a future date. Or that was what he told me happened.

Roby said he set up three more times for Nussbeck to come in for his deposition. But every time there was something way more important that the defendant had to do, and they were cancelled.

Then one day, out of the blue at one of our many meetings, Roby laid a piece of paper on the table before me called a Stipulation for Compromise Settlement. The document read that there would be $861.04 weekly compensation and the Second Injury Fund was going to pick up an additional $451.02 a week for my previous injury. Wow! What a sweet deal! I took a quick picture of the document with my phone when Roby left the room for a minute. I wanted a copy of the greatest news I had received in years.

In October and November, we had five depositions scheduled and five meetings cancelled. But Roby was more concerned about getting that check from the work comp case settlement to me. It would take a couple of weeks for the insurance company to even cut the check. Roby said that those insurance companies like to hold that money as long as they can. "That's what they always do," said Roby.

A couple more weeks passed with no word from Roby. Then he called and said that he finally received the check in the mail. But he first had to get his partner to sign the check. And he thought it would be a better idea, if he deposited it into their account at the law office so that I didn't have to wait for the 10 days to get my money. He was going to do me a favor because he knew how eager I was to finally get my money.

Another week went by, and I was getting impatient. I had been waiting for some kind of justice and compensation for over five years. What was taking so long? Then, Roby emailed me on a Friday morning, saying he was bringing the check over to my house that night after he left work. It got to be 10PM. He never showed up and didn't answer his phone.

All this time, I had been keeping my cousin Rick informed about the progression of the cases. This guy, after all this was his boy, his trainee, at his office. Over a month before this time, I had sent Rick a copy of a post off Facebook. A lady stated in her post that Eric Roby was a thief and a liar. He had messed up her case something horribly and was alerting people to beware of this lawyer fraud!

The post had been forwarded to me by my daughter, Maria. Who was also scammed by Roby during my ordeal. The warning signs were becoming brighter now. But Rick wasn't impressed however at the "hearsay" and laughed it off. He said, "Don't believe something you read on Facebook." We were into our fifth year going on six and still no closure in either case? I wrote a response email to Rick. Telling him about all the cancellations and that Roby had been holding onto my check for weeks now. I wanted the money, and I wanted him to investigate what was going on around in his law office. I had lost my wife because of his protégé buddy, and I wanted some answers.

What did Rick do? Took my email and handed it directly to his buddy, Roby to read. Then Rick called and explained to me that Roby admitted to him that he really didn't have the check just yet. He was just telling me that so I would calm down. He told Rick that knew how desperate I was, but he expected the check to show any day now. All was good and he had this case and the work comp case all under control. Rick just needed to calm me down. Roby was getting nervous of my behavior.

Rick bought every bit of his lies from his dear friend and told me I was overreacting.

Eric was a good lawyer and doing a fine job with this case.

In the coming weeks, more depositions were scheduled and cancelled. The civil case was to go to court on the 11th of November. Roby told me that it was cancelled. I don't remember his excuse that time.

I called Roby and told him to be at the law office at 10:00am on the 21st.

I walked in the building and headed downstairs where Roby was in the downstairs conference room rummaging around in a box with papers. I approached him and asked, "Where's my money?"

Roby said, "Its upstairs on the girl's desk."

I said, "Go get it, now! I'm done messing with you!" As I got within inches of his face.

My loud voice carried out of the room. Because in walked Bill Hall, a senior member of the law firm. Hall asked, "What is going on in here?"

I said to him, "This son of a bitch has been lying to me for five years. I want my money, and he said he has it!"

Hall asked me. "Well, who are you?" I exclaimed, "I'm Ricks cousin, Mark! I was introduced to you over four years ago, Bill. I've been in this law office two days a week for the last five years. You're telling me you don't recognize me? Where's my money?"

I then pulled out my phone and showed him the various text messages from Roby. Especially the one telling me he has the settlement check. And the text saying he would deliver it to my house that Friday night.

Hall was reading the emails on my phone as Roby peered over his shoulder wide eyed. Hall then said, "Give me your number and I'll get back with you." I wrote my name and number on a piece of paper and handed it to him.

A couple of days passed. No word yet, so I made a call to the law office and asked the receptionist for Bill Hall.

Hall answered, "How are you Mr. Scaletty?

I answered, "Not too good Bill. What have you found out?"

Bill replied. "We have a problem here. I have notified our insurance carrier and the other partners. I will have to get back with you at some point."

I replied, "You don't know what problems you have yet, Bill. But you're gonna' find out."

Bill and I haven't spoken since that day, or Roby.

The Riddle: What does a liar do when he's dead?

The Answer: He lies still.

A dead body, no matter who it was when alive, will "lie still" and no longer move. A dead liar, however, won't just "lie still" in that sense- they'll also "lie still" in that their lies will continue until the truth is presented.

I want the truth!

20LF-CR00577

PROBABLE CAUSE STATEMENT FORM

Date: 07/15/20

I, Detective Ray Burns, knowing that false statements on this form are punishable by law, state that the facts contained herein are true.

OCN:

1. I have probable cause to believe that, Eric D. Roby, DOB: 08/18/78, SSN: 488-92-3156, living at 1203 Ben St., Buckner, Missouri 64016, may have committed one or more criminal offenses.

2. The facts supporting this belief are: In the year of 2017 two individuals identified as HMD and CLS were involved in a civil suit against the city of Odessa, Missouri. These two individuals hired an attorney identified as Eric D. Roby to represent them in the civil suit. The civil suit involved a sewer and drainage problem on the property of HMD and CLS. In April of 2019 Eric Roby met with HMD and CLS and informed both of these individuals that the city of Odessa had agreed to resolve the sewer and drainage problem on their properties and that Lafayette County Judge Dennis Rolf had signed the legal document. Mr. Roby gave both HMD and CLS a copy of the document alleged to have been signed by Judge Rolf. After reviewing the document provided to them by Eric Roby both HMD and CLS believed they were successful in their civil suit against the city of Odessa, Missouri. HMD wanted to get a copy of the report on file so he contacted the Lafayette County Circuit Clerks Office and was informed that the civil suit against the city of Odessa Missouri had been dismissed with prejudice. HMD informed the representative from the circuit clerk's office that he had in his possession an amended order signed by Judge Rolf. The clerk asked HMD to send a copy of this document to the circuit clerk's Office. HMD then contacted CLS and she sent an email message of the document that both HMD and CLS had received from attorney Eric Roby. After receiving this document the employee at the circuit clerk's office who was familiar with the signature of Judge Rolf determined that the signature on this document was not the signature of Judge Dennis Rolf.
    On June 12, 2020 I made contact with Judge Dennis Rolf and showed him a copy of the legal document that HMD and CLS stated they had both received by their attorney Eric Roby. Judge Rolf stated that the signature on this document was not his signature and was a forgery.
    On June 22, 2020 I made contact with Mr. Eric Roby at his residence in Buckner Missouri. I allowed Mr. Roby to view the document with the signature on the fifth page of this document. This was the same document that both HMD and CLS state they had received from Mr. Roby. According to Mr. Roby, he did not give this document to either HMD or CLS and he had not signed this document using the name of Judge Dennis Rolf.
    It is believed at this time that Eric D. Roby is responsible for the forgery on the legal document that he provided to both HMD and CLS.

3. Felony / Misdemeanor

PROBABLE CAUSE STATEMENT FORM

A. I believe the defendant will not appear in court in response to a criminal Summons because: Due to the serious nature of this offense there is probable cause to believe that the defendant will not appear to answer charges from a summons and a warrant for the defendant is necessary.

B. I believe the defendant poses:

    1. A danger to a crime victim because: Defendant is acquainted with both HMD and CLS and is aware of the location where both of these individuals reside.

    2. A danger to the community or to any other person because:

Detective Ray Burns #138
Print Name

Ray Burns
Signature

CHAPTER 10

FORSAKEN

After spending over sixty plus months with your lawyer you think you know them well. A trust is formed, and a relationship, whether it be personal or professional develops. The good times, the bad times, laughing together and even sharing the sadness at my mother and my brother's death during this lengthy ordeal.

I did that with my cousin, Rick and his intern, Eric. Whose name changed to just plain "Roby" when we were into our fourth year together.

I never liked Roby particularly, and my gut told me not to trust him. But I second guessed myself and trusted my cousin to help me. But the great prosecutor, Richard P. Scaletty, completely fooled me, he betrayed me, and helped his intern with his horrendous acts of malpractice out of his own office right under his nose. Even though Roby lied to him, to my wife, his own firm, and me, Rick has never apologized for any of it. Even though he was the person that set the whole deal up.

So now what was I to do? Call the cops? Call another Lawyer? Release my biker brothers. Or call in the Mob? All these things were running through my mind.

I was injured at a workplace that was unsafe! Injured by reckless illegals and their disregard for any workplace safety practices that were put in place and agreed to by them. My "boss" discriminated against me numerous ways after I was injured. Demoting me and then creating a hostile workplace against me. Then fired me after 6 months of his bullshit setup that left me with no income or insurance offered.

My wife had even left me because of the tension from the lies and disinformation that Rick and Roby created. Roby even suggested and tried convincing me to take matters into my own hands a few times. He said he was frustrated with what he told me they were doing, and I should go beat them up. Saying they were the ones doing all the stalling, when really it was all him.

My $1400.00 house payment was due along with the $250.00 electric bill and water bill. Matt was still going to college and needed funds that I did not have. All this time I have been praying that the money would show up and this nightmare would finally be over. But now I felt I was back to square one. Alone.

I thought I had done excellent preparation and note keeping for this case. I had given Roby boxes of evidence I had on these roofing crooks. My records and daily job reports, emails and pictures of documentation were all stacked somewhere at the law office in a box. I knew Hall didn't have a clue what his employee was doing.

But by now I had learned one thing; Not to trust anyone, especially lawyers.

I kept copies of every email and copies of all the incriminating pictures. I even said that in the deposition, when Wiedner, their lawyer asked me where I had them stored. I told him in a safe place. He really did want those incriminating pictures of their workers in unsafe acts. They were a great admission of guilt and that all my statements were true about their unsafe practices. But even though I had all the evidence about who and why I was suing, I now had to fight against the S.O.B. that was supposed to be helping me against them. I knew Rick was conversing with his crony lawyer buddies, and some kind of chatter was going on at his office. They were looking to distant themselves from Roby and save their ass. They had to come up with a play that protected this from going public. To hide their mistakes.

I never felt so forsaken and abandon in my life. I needed to be very rational about this situation I was thrown in. Not rush into how my gut was telling me to do. Why that would be a crime, and their plan. To push me to react and do something out of anger so they could get rid of me.

They wanted to keep their money safe and unethical secrets from getting out anymore that it had.

Feeling so close to being done with this whole five-and-a-half-year ordeal, and now I was just starting over. I needed to figure this mess out, but my mind was racing in every direction.

I took a deep breath. I looked up 'Legal Malpractice Attorneys'. There were just a few listed that I found in Kansas City. I wrote basically the same email to each of them. Stating the case numbers that I had, with Roby's contact information along with my own. I knew a smart attorney could verify that information.

I also sent a similar email to the Missouri Attorneys' Generals office in Jefferson City, asking for their help. I believed they could tell I was desperate, since I gave them a little background on what I had been going through for the last five and a half years with Roby. I hit the 'send' button, shook my head and waited.

The next day I received an email from one law office saying they were more into medical malpractice than legal stuff, so they weren't interested. Strike one. Then I got a phone call from another law firm I sent the letter to. They asked me if I was related to Rick Scaletty. I said, "Yeah, he's my first cousin, unfortunately." So of course, they didn't want to prosecute a fraternity brother, so they declined. Strike two. I was starting to realize that this family of lawyers were a much tighter family, than I was being a first cousin to Rick. I was realizing this band of brothers was hard to crack.

Another day passed. I received a phone call from a woman named Tina. She had a pleasant voice and said that her lawyers had researched my case and she was with a firm that did exactly what I was looking for. Tina asked me if I could come to their law office located downtown in the Crown Center district at my convenience. I said sure and made an appointment for two days later.

The 2345 Grand building was a huge skyscraper overlooking Crown Center and the famous Union Station. The Carter Law Offices were on the sixteenth floor of this massive glass building that contained mostly law offices of big firms. I had to pass through a security station stating my business and with whom, before even entering the elevator.

As I walked through the door entering their suite, the view of the city was magnificent with the floor to ceiling windows stretching all the way across the length of the various offices. Tina Carter, sat as the receptionist and welcomed me in by name. She told me to have a seat in any of the four plush brown leather chairs in the reception area and Doug would be right out. There were many hints of a golf lover around. On the walls were pictures of golf courses and there were golf magazines on the end tables. I loved golf. I had turned pro in 1983, and even played on two mini tours and competed in tournaments around the Midwest and even on the REMAX World Long Drive competition numerous times. My many golf bags sat in the corner at home now. Just tearful reminders of what I was capable of before my injury.

From out of an office door down the hall walked a big man. He looked to be a bit younger than I, and he was probably 6'1" and 250. He introduced himself as Doug Carter, the senior partner. Through another office door, came another man, and introduced himself as Jon McCoy. Another lawyer with the firm. He was younger, probably 45, and 6'4" with an athletic body. Both were sharply dressed though not wearing suits. Dressed more like golfers. I liked that.

Mr. Carter suggested we go into his office and talk. We all headed down the hallway, even Tina. I soon found out, Tina was his wife and Legal Assistant. We all took seats in the office except for Tina. She stood off to the side as Mr. Carter began to speak.

"Mr. Scaletty, we have reviewed your case," said Mr. Carter. "First off call me Doug." I replied, "And I'm Mark." Doug said, "Jon and I have gone over the case that Eric Roby was representing for you. Did you know that your civil case was Dismissed years ago? And your Workmen's Compensation case has yet to even been filled?

Now there I was sitting in a room with four people I just met, and never felt so alone. I clenched my fist and felt ill. "Fucking Roby," I said under my breath. My stomach ached as I sat and looked down at the floor. Hoping not to show the people I had just been introduced to my pain, my anger and feelings of complete isolation and abandonment. Together we had a long journey ahead, and no one in that room knew then, what the truth was and the mess they would uncover. But I had to trust them. It was all I had.

CHAPTER 11

REALIZING REALITY

As I sat in my new counsel's office, I was hopeful they would help me. But in reality I couldn't bring myself to completely trust them. They were lawyers, and members of the same club of liars, thieves and manipulators as the rest of them. I didn't trust any lawyer now. Nor the courts, judges or the system they represented. At this particular time in my life, I didn't really trust the sun would ever shine again. But what other choice did I have now. My whole career had been brought to a halt and I was forced into retirement. My family life with my new wife, our dream house, and thoughts of retirement at sixty-five were now in the past. I wasn't even able to enjoy playing golf again. Even from the forward tees with the other short hitters, I couldn't swing the club hard enough to barely make it past the Red Tee Box.

Doug and Jon began to explain what they thought could have happened. They both exclaimed they had never seen a law office be so reckless and careless in their handling of a case. Doug explained that law offices with multiple partners have their calendars linked together. All the attorneys in the firm would be alerted on what upcoming cases and task the lawyers would be required to do. A failure free system that would notify all the other lawyers about upcoming or pending actions that would need attention. Such as discoveries, depositions, hearings, court appearances or meeting with the judge. Anything pertaining to any case would be sent to all the lawyers in the firm. This helps to ensure that nothing gets missed. Why was there was nothing in place at Rick's office to catch the various felonious acts repeated many times against myself and other clients was still a mystery.

Roby had been committing crimes against clients for over five years.

I was just the first one to put it all together and bring attention to the issues going on at Rick's law office. Now they were scrambling to subdue the whole thing. They sure didn't want this knucklehead bringing the whole firm down, or this scandal getting to the press. The senior partners were going to have to pull some of their lawyer tricks out of the bag for protection against the truth getting out.

Doug went on to explain, that Roby, purposely missed filling motions, missed filing interrogatories, missed pretrial conferences and more. The case filed in 2016 was dismissed with prejudice. The Case.net docket entries for the 2018 case with three motions for Sanctions were dismissed with prejudice by the judge due to Roby's incompetence. The case 1616CV14931, Mark Scaletty V Aspen Contracting Inc. was now closed. I was never told, and Roby kept stringing me along.

Aspen was off the hook for everything that happened along with everything they did. Everything! There was no going back on them. They got away with discrimination and retaliation due to my incompetent lawyer. Roby's incompetence almost killed me with the heart issues caused by the stress he inflicted. Aspen was free from prosecution and still mistreating other employees as they had me. Three of their previous employees even contacted me, when they found out about my lawsuit. They called me and told me of the discrimination they were experiencing at Aspen by Nussbeck. I told Roby and he felt they could help my case. I gave all their contact information to Roby to set up interviews, but Roby never gave any of them a call, sent an email or made any attempt to contact them. Roby feared Nussbeck and his hired gun attorney. It was evident he was intimidated by the way he would shake when we talked about them. Roby was a coward!

The Supreme Court of Missouri, SC98358, was the Motion for Suspension for Roby. He had finally been reprimanded after deceiving over ten other clients including my daughter, Maria. But him getting kicked out of his little law club was the least of my worries. I had much bigger fish to fry, and I wanted Rick's ass along with his bull shit law firm he had made millions with 20 years ago.

This was going to take some doing said Doug. We have what is called, "A case within a case." With Aspen off the hook, we must go after the law firm that was supposed to be representing you. We must prove your case, it's value and show that Roby completely misrepresented you. The second part was easy. It was all well documented on Case.net. as to what Roby had done, or not done. We just needed to justify the million-dollar lawsuit against Aspen. The case against the law firm and Roby was the easy part to prove. No one likes crooked lawyers more than a jury that's summoned to court. I wanted that day of reckoning to come more than anything.

Rick, of course, was laying low in hiding all this time. Probably left the country again to avoid any questioning by the senior partners that were supposed to be watching over Rick's trainee. Rick was always good at disappearing when things got rough or difficult. He would weasel out and leave it to the partners to figure it out. The other lawyers at the firm were unaware that I had sent Rick notice and proof months before. Alerting him about Roby's lies and deceit with my settlement payment fiasco along with the Facebook statements about Roby. There were so many secrets in that firm that needed to be exposed, and I was determined to get the truth out and for the guilty to be recognized. I could only hope that Doug and Jon were committed to justice and bringing some of their own lawyer bros to face the consequences. That is what I hired them for.

I went to various meetings at Carter's office to discuss the many events that occurred with Roby. I signed releases for subpoenas to retrieve all my documents that I had at Rick's office. This part took a couple of months for Carter Law Office to put together. The finally, an inch and a half thick, Enclosure To Settlement Letter Dated May 5, 2020, was ready. It read, Insureds: Eric Roby and McElligott, Ewan & Hall, P.C. Claim No: 115200, Policy No: 0000060-2019(LPL-MO-FUL)

• Case.net docket entries for the case

- 2016 Petition
- Dismissal of 2016 Petion
- Case.net docket entries for the 2018 case
- 2018 Petition
- Three Motions for Sanctions with Suggestions filed in the 2018 case
- Judge Rolland's Order dismissing the 2018 case with prejudice
- Falsified Stipulation of Compromise Settlement presented to Mr. Scaletty
- Motion of Chief Disciplinary Counsel for Emergency Suspension of Eric Roby
- Order of Missouri Supreme Court for Emergency Suspension of Eric Roby
- Fee Awards from Carter Law Offices' last five employment cases resolved by trial or arbitration
- A list of names and addresses of health care providers who provided treatment to or evaluated Mr. Scaletty for injuries suffered from the date of injury until the date of this demand, together with HIPAA compliant written authorizations
- A list of the names and addresses of all of Mr. Scaletty's employers at the time Mr. Scaletty was first injured until the date of this demand, together with written authorizations
- Reports of reflecting verdicts in recent MHRA case. (Note: Additional sums were or will be awarded for statutory attorney fees, cost and litigation expenses
- Report of Daniel J. Welsh, C.P.A.
- Affidavit of Mark Scaletty
- Statement of Carrie Scaletty

This Enclosure laid out the undeniable evidence that no one could dispute.

Here is the statement that my wife, Carrie submitted:

I met Mark in December of 2011, and we officially began dating in February of 2012. He was happy go lucky and we always managed to find fun things to do. On any given weekend, you might find us camping, going to dinner, dancing, going to a concert, or one of his son's sporting events. Life was good and promising.

In December of 2013, Mark proposed. We had plans for our retirement, traveling to see the various sites around the US, making memories.

In April/ May timeframe of 2014, Mark was offered a job with Aspen Roofing. He left the security of his Kansas City Kansas public school job to work for Aspen Roofing. They made all the right promises of an alluring salary. While working for Aspen, he was sent to Washington State to work on a job at the Mount Saint Helen's Visitor center. (Sept/ Oct 2014 timeframe) It was there, he was injured on the job, tearing his rotator cuff and several tears/ rips in the bicep muscle. Little did I realize how drastically our life would change because of this injury.

Mark was in constant pain and could barely raise his arm. Certainly not enough to swing dance anymore.

He was put into a commissioned sales position for Aspen in about November of 2014. Not many roofs to be repaired in the middle of winter. No commission, no income. Money was tight. I'm not sure how he survived. His mood was less than happy.

In May of 2015, we moved into our "new to us" home in Lee's Summit. (I sold my home in Olathe and Mark was in the process of selling his home in Lee' Summit). At the time we were trying to purchase the Lee's Summit home, the lender would not approve Mark for the home loan, so I secured it in my name only. (adding him to the deed later).

We were married in June of 2015.

July 2015, Mark was scheduled to have his rotator cuff surgery, FINALLY. Only nine months after his injury. We thought this would get things back on an even keel so to speak. We arrived at the surgery center, they took him back and let me know I would be called back in about 30 minutes, to see him before surgery. Well, 45 minutes later still no call back......finally I was called back to see him, only to learn his heart rate was extremely high and he needed to go to the emergency room immediately. Basically he was a walking stroke victim...just waiting for it to happen.

So, we get to the ER and find out his health insurance (provided by Aspen) was no longer good. So, $300 (out of pocket) and he was admitted to the ER. They gave him an injection to get the heart rate down, and he was released to go home......however, before released. He was scheduled to see a cardiologist.

We made several visits to the cardiologist (Dr Bloom), over the months of July and August. Lots of test and EKG's. On September 1st, Mark had a procedure to shock his heart back into rhythm. He was put on heart medication and blood thinners.

Our life was a constant parade of doctor visits. Not exactly the type of social life we were planning on.

In December 2015 Mark finally had his rotator cuff/ bicep repair surgery. He was still in a lot of pain, and some days would sit in his recliner, eyes closed, all day long. Not having anything to say, didn't want to eat anything, was despondent.

All the while, during the timeframe from Oct/Nov 2014 until December 2015, he was also making frequent visits to Eric Roby's office. We were under the impression that the civil case against Aspen was progressing, as well as the processing of his Workman's comp case. By December 2015, it had been a full year since Mark had received any income to speak of. He was getting Social Security, but that's not much compared to what he had been making.

I was making the house payment, buying groceries, buying or making Christmas presents for his children and grandchildren, along with mine. (at that time, I believe we had 16 grandchildren between the two of us).

This trend continued through all of 2016, 2017, 2018 and part of 2019. Even though Mark started receiving his Sheet Metal Workers pension, and a little from KPERS. The bulk of the financial burden was left to me.

We no longer went out dancing, we only took one vacation between Nov 2014 and mid-June 2019, and even then, we were led to believe the Workman's Comp settlement was coming soon.

I can't begin to recall the numbers of times we were just about to leave the house for an appointment with Eric Roby, and Mark's phone would ring.....sure enough, it would be Eric calling to postpone the meeting for one reason or another. It was ridiculous. Everything was pushed out further and further....depositions, meetings, supposed settlements with Aspen.....all the promises of a settlement became nothing but cheap words. The frustration was horrible. It wasn't Mark's fault, but it didn't make the day to day living easier.

I should also add that I had to start taking medication for high blood pressure during this time. I've never been bothered by that before. The stress was difficult for both of us. We've lived with the stress and pressure of this situation for nearly 5 and a half years.

Certainly not the way I intended to spend my "golden" years.

In June of 2019, I decided I could no longer live the day-to-day stress of all of this. I moved back to Olathe and our divorce hearing will take place as soon as the courts are open again. So, I'd say the injury and the court cases taking forever, and then finding out the civil case had been mismanaged....well, that's a lot to deal with. Mark's a decent man, he doesn't deserve the treatment he's received from Aspen, nor from his attorney, Eric Roby. I pray he gets the settlement he so rightly is entitled to.

Sincerely, Carrie Scaletty

The evidence was overwhelming in my favor against Roby and Aspen. Would it be enough?

Supreme Court of Missouri
en banc

August 11, 2020

In re: Eric D. Roby,	)	
	)	
Respondent.	)	Supreme Court No. SC98550
	)	MBE # 56582
	)	

ORDER

The Chief Disciplinary Counsel having filed an information advising this Court of its findings, after investigation, that there is probable cause to believe Respondent, Eric D. Roby, is guilty of professional misconduct; and

The Chief Disciplinary Counsel having filed with said information, pursuant to Rule 5.13, a notice of default, notifying the Court that Respondent, Eric D. Roby, failed to timely file an answer or other response within the time required although Respondent was properly served;

Therefore, pursuant to Rule 5.13, Respondent is in default.

Further, the Chief Disciplinary Counsel having filed a recommendation for discipline; and

Respondent having failed to respond to the same;

It appearing Respondent is guilty of professional misconduct as a result of violations of Rules 4-1.1, 4-1.3, 4-1.4, and 4-8.4(c) and should be disciplined;

Now, therefore, it is ordered by this Court that the said Eric D. Roby be, and he is hereby disbarred, that his right and license to practice law in the State of Missouri is canceled and that his name be stricken from the roll of attorneys in this State.

It is further ordered that the said Respondent comply in all respects with Rule 5.27 – Procedure Following a Disbarment or Suspension Order.

Fee pursuant to Rule 5.19(h) in the amount of $2,000.00 payable to the Clerk of this Court to the credit of the Advisory Committee Fund taxed to Respondent.

Costs taxed to Respondent.

Day - to - Day

George W. Draper III
Chief Justice

OFFICE OF CHIEF DISCIPLINARY COUNSEL   OCDC

SUPREME COURT OF MISSOURI

3327 AMERICAN AVENUE
JEFFERSON CITY, MISSOURI 65109-1016
PHONE: (573) 635-7400
FAX: (573) 635-2240

August 21, 2020

Mr. Mark Scaletty
3816 SW Lido Drive
Lee's Summit, MO 64082

Re: **Eric Roby, File No. 19-1589-IV**

Dear Mr. Scaletty:

As you know, you have a complaint pending with this office against Eric Roby. This is to advise you that on August 11, 2020, the Missouri Supreme Court issued an order disbarring Mr. Roby from the practice law for ethical misconduct. A copy of the Court's Order is enclosed herewith. At this time, we are closing the investigative file regarding your complaint. Should Mr. Roby attempt to apply for reinstatement at any time in the future, we will contact you and complete our investigation.

If you believe that you have been financially damaged as a result of the conduct of Mr. Roby, you may make a claim for reimbursement of the damages that you suffered from the Client Security Fund administered by The Missouri Bar. You may contact the Fund through the Missouri Bar, P.O. Box 119, Jefferson City, MO 65102-0119.

Sincerely,

Alan D. Pratzel
Chief Disciplinary Counsel

ADP
Enclosure

Mark Scaletty

IN THE CIRCUIT COURT OF LAFAYETTE COUNTY, MISSOURI
ASSOCIATE DIVISION
COMPLAINT

STATE OF MISSOURI	)	PA File No. 107024908
Plaintiff,	)	
	)	
vs.	)	Case No.
	)	OCN:
Eric Damen Roby	)	
1203 Ben Street	)	W/ M DOB: 08/18/1978
Buckner, MO 64016	)	
	)	SSN: 488-92-3156
Defendant.	)	

COUNT: I

The Prosecuting Attorney for the County of Lafayette, State of Missouri, upon information and belief, charges the defendant in violation of Section 570.090, RSMo, committed the class D felony of forgery, punishable upon conviction under Sections 558.002 and 558.011, RSMo, in that between April 1, 2019 and April 30, 2019, in the County of Lafayette, State of Missouri, the defendant, with the purpose to defraud, transferred with the knowledge or belief that it would be used as genuine, a writing, namely, a Lafayette County Circuit Court Amended Order, knowing that it had been made, so that it purported to have a genuineness that it did not possess.

Charge Code: 570.090-001Y20172589.0

RANGE OF PUNISHMENT: Class A Felony -- 10 to 30 years or life imprisonment in the Missouri Department of Corrections. Class B Felony – 5 to 15 years in the Missouri Department of Corrections. Class C Felony – 3 to 10 years in the Missouri Department of Corrections, and/or up to a $10,000 fine. Class D Felony – 1 to 7 years in the Missouri Department of Corrections, and/or up to 1 year in the County Jail and/or up to a $10,000.00 fine. Class E Felony – 1 to 4 years in the Missouri Department of Corrections, or up to 1 year in the County Jail and/or up to a $10,000.00 fine.

The facts that form the basis for this information and belief are contained in the attached statement(s) of facts concerning this matter, which statement(s) are made a part hereof and are submitted herewith as a basis upon which this court may find the existence of probable cause for the issuance of the warrant.

Wherefore, the Prosecuting Attorney prays that a summons be issued as provided by law.

/s/KRISTEN ELLIS HILBRENNER,
KRISTEN ELLIS HILBRENNER, #58824
Prosecuting Attorney
County of Lafayette
Telephone-(660)259-6181

CHAPTER 12

THE EAGLE FLUTTERS

My new counsel, Jon McCoy and Doug Carter, started educating me on what Roby had done. They said that on June 21, 2016, Roby did file a lawsuit.

The next day, Judge Marco A. Rowland, was assigned to hear the case against Aspen Contracting. On July 21, 2016, Aspen was served with a summons. In the next two months, Aspen filed Pro Hac Vice and Order Granting Leave. They were trying to pin this whole thing on me. Aspen wanted discovery to prove this whole thing was my fault. In a Work Comp case there is no guilty party. But that wasn't going to be good enough for Aspen. They wanted revenge against me and Roby for even challenging them. On November 9th, 2016, there was a jury trial scheduled, with a trial date of September 18, 2017, at 9:00am. Expected length of trial: 4 days. But Roby did not inform me about this, or any of the proceedings that were taking place.

On August 30th, 2017, there was a pre-trail conference scheduled. Roby did not attend or tell me or let me know about a conference. On September 7th, 2017, there was another hearing that was canceled by Roby. He never informed about that one either. Between then and August of 2019, there were Affidavits, Orders and Interrogatories that were filed that Roby never informed me about. The case was dropped by Judge Roland on September 26th, 2019, with prejudice because of Roby's incompetence and failure to follow up. Why did he hide this information? Because he was in too deep with lies and had skeletons in every closet.

Carter explained all of this to me and how Roby and his firm had dropped the ball on every aspect of this lawsuit. Now it was up to him and Jon to prove the case that Roby screwed up. The lawsuit Carter Law was pursuing would prove that the Defendant, Pat Nussbeck had created a hostile environment based on my disability and altered the terms, privileges and condition of my employment. As a direct and proximate result of the unlawful conduct, I suffered damages which included emotional distress, pain and suffering, physical injury, past and future wage and benefits, a detrimental job record, career damage and diminished career potential, mental distress in the form of embarrassment, degradation, humiliation, anxiety, loss of enjoyment of life, loss of sleep, and other non-pecuniary losses. I was also entitled to other appropriate equitable relief. And entitled to recover all my expenses, cost, expert witness fees and attorney's fees in this matter as well as other appropriate equitable relief. That was just Count One.

Count Two was about the retaliation. (Missouri Statue Section 287.780) No employer or agent shall discharge or in any way discriminate against any employee for exercising any rights under this chapter. Any employee who has been discharged or discriminated against shall have a civil action for damages against his employer. Aspen was clearly in violation of the law, and Carter would prove it.

Between November 12, 2019, and February 11, 2020, the Missouri Attorney General had received ten complaints about Roby and initiated investigations into Respondent's alleged conduct. This was relating to his representation of clients between June 2019 and February 2020, as found in complaint 19-1706-IV in the Sixteenth Circuit Court of Jackson County, Missouri.

The facts of the various complaints showed that Roby engaged in serious professional misconduct. Providing his clients with various fraudulent documents related to court matters. It was in the publics interest to prohibit Roby to practice law. Then finally, on February 11th, 2020, Roby was disbarred.

I couldn't believe all this had transpired right in front of me. Roby had screwed me over along with so many other clients. Now Carter had his work ahead of him. To prove Roby was a con man was easy. To prove that Aspen had discriminated against me was documented. I wanted my day in court. I wanted to tell my story to the judge and jury and let them decide who was guilty.

It took months to get my paperwork and records from Roby's office. Bill Hall, the senior partner had no idea what Roby had been doing, let alone where all the documents were at the law office. They were going to drag their feet for as long as legally possible working on a game plan.

Doug was getting the evidence in order. He was ready to take on Hall, the firm and their lawyer. Even Hall couldn't answer for himself about what happened in his own office. Cousin Rick was nowhere to be found, of course. He stayed low like the snake he is. Rick was informed about what was going on but wasn't going down for his friend that got caught. That was his mistake.

On May 5, 2020, Carter Law filed the Enclosures to Settlement against McElliigott, Ewan & Hall, P.C... Just like fishing, it was time to wait and see what was offered.

As my luck would have it in this case, Doug informed me that the law firm was saying that Roby hadn't signed an insurance release form for that year. Doug said that there is a form that lawyers sign yearly stating they are of sound mind and body, and they would never do any harm to a client or the firm. Well, we know every lawyer lies on that form every year. These slimy S.O.B.'s were going to try every trick they could to not pay a penny for committing a crime. More lawyer tricks and trying to find any reason not to be held responsible.

Carter was able to do some investigating, and his sources found that Roby had signed the form, so that trick didn't work. But Hall had more smoke and mirrors to show and divert attention away from him. We discovered that their insurance company had a million-dollar cap on any claims against them. And to make it more undesirable for us, any fees for their defense would come off that cap. Carter figured that Hall would spend around $250,000.00 to defend the firm and himself. Carter said that it would cost about the same for his fees, leaving a half million dollars for me. Carter would get forty percent of the gross amount that was recovered if the matter settled without any litigation being filed; and fifty percent of the gross amount that is recovered after litigation is filed. But I also had to pay all the expenses incurred. Including court filing fees, deposition transcript cost, video production charges, cost charged to obtain records and fees charged by expert witnesses or attorneys who would testify or consult at request.

It still didn't look redeemable for me. I was getting screwed any way it went down.

Carter didn't want to take the case to court. He felt it would take over a year to get a court date, since the courts were still backed up from the Covid scam. He felt we should pressure Hall and go for as much money as we could get out of the old bastard. So that's what I reluctantly agreed to. Carter sent Hall a letter saying we would drop the case if he paid up.

Now for me it's just a simple math problem. I was making close to a hundred thousand a year with benefits at the Kansas City Kansas School District. I went to Aspen with the assurance from Larry Hadley, that with my resume of extensive metal roofing experience that I would make $150,000.00 a year with Aspen. We know now that Larry Hadley lied about the money along with my duties, so let's just use the $100,000.00 a year commission to make it easy math. Eight years equals $800,000.00 and is what I lost during this time. That amount would be owed to me for my injury and compensation let alone the pain and suffering I experienced. That amount doesn't even include the thousands out of pocket during those years or the cost of losing my wife, house and career. But that wasn't even close to what Hall offered. Is that a surprise? Carter got his cut and I had to pay income tax on the total amount. The IRS considered it income and they don't care that I had to hire someone else to recoup my loss. After everything I had been through would you expect me to be mad?

My forty plus years of experience as a Master Sheet Metal Worker my compensation for losing everything as well as my dignity, my award was reduced to peanuts after taxes. The lawyers and the court system with the fictitious judges won this game. I still had nothing but expenses and bills from the last eight most miserable and painful years of my life. I can't play golf, ride my motorcycle or even hold my grandkids without being in constant pain. My shoulder ached so severely it has prevented me from ever getting a peaceful night's sleep for almost nine years now, but I'm supposed to feel compensated.

My oldest son, Todd, had relocated from Missouri and bought a mobile home in Interlachen, Florida around 2012. I had kept him advised of how Rick screwed me and set me up with Roby. He had heard additional information from his sister, Maria about the shady dealings going on with Roby. Since 1974, I had raised Todd from the time he was 18 months old, after his mother left him next door with a neighbor. I was in the Marine Corps during that time. Todd was raised around my many motorcycle club friends and the ways we did business then with enemies. He didn't get his first haircut until he was five, almost six. He would ride between my legs holding onto the gas tank of one of my choppers, as we pulled into the preschool parking lot. Todd knew I still had plenty of contacts with lots of bad dudes that I could call. Just say the word and I could have any one of them ripped from their house and drug behind a pickup down a gravel road attached by a log chain. He knew I was livid about the way I had been treated and he feared I would take matters into my own hands soon. Roby wanted me to retaliate but now he was the victim. Todd had seen me take care of problems before when I had a beef with someone. We talked a few times about what remedy I had for them, and he was adamant to get me away from Kansas City and them before I acted on it.

But I couldn't leave Kansas City just yet. I was still taking care of my elderly mother and had been for over 15 years since my dad died. I had moved my mother from their home after my father passed and found a nice facility called Villa Ventura in south Kansas City. She had many other widowed friends from her church family that resided there. She had a nice apartment there was comfortable. I came over to visit her a few times a week, also taking her to doctor appointments, doing her laundry, bringing her store items she needed and taking care of her finances. I was the only person in my family doing anything for her, so leaving was not an option. My mom knew well of all the problems I was having at her nephew, Rick's office, as we spoke about it often. I told her everything about what was happening. My mother was a saint. I never heard her speak bad about anyone. But she despised Rick for his part in what he did to Maria and me.

Todd finally convinced me to fly to Florida to at least check it out and take a look at things. I had never been to Florida in my life. Never had given the place much thought. I had lived in Pheonix, Tucson and Las Vegas. Loved the Southwest. I hated rain, bugs, and humidity, but I went to see anyway. I had to make up a story that I had the flu to tell my mom why I wouldn't be coming by for the next few days just to have time to even make the trip to Florida.

I flew into Orlando. What a traffic joke that place is! I drove north a couple of hours to Interlachen, where Todd's place was located. In the next four days we put over 1500 miles on my rental car just driving around checking places out that I had found interesting on Zillow as a prospective residence. I had found one place that had two acres and needed some handy man work I was capable of handling. It was owned by a married couple that were getting divorced and she got the house. I made a cash offer that she took. I now had a place to retire when the time came to get out of KC Missery.

When I returned to Kansas City, I went to see mom. She was furious that I left town without telling her the truth. But I told her I had a nice visit with Todd, and that cooled her down for a little bit. She became very sick not too long after my trip. I was by her side for days as she fell into decline. Her 98-year-old body was tired, and she passed on March 20th of

2021. She donated her body to K.U. Medical Center for research. We had a beautiful service at her Catholic church of Christ the King and there were many nieces and nephews, friends and the children of parents that my mom had been friends with for decades. Most of their parents had passed already, so the children showed respect as I had, attending many funerals in my family's name since my mother was too frail to attend them.

Rick was not in attendance at the church mass. Abroad somewhere again is my guess. However, he did send two huge flower arrangements, letting the attendees know who had the bucks and could spend the most on flowers. Typical Rick style.

After my mom had passed, I had to empty her apartment and sort through her belongings. I donated her furniture to the Goodwill and bank visits to take care of her financial things. About a month and half went by and I was ready to get the hell out of Kansas City and away from the lawyer drama I had been going through with Roby. Carter Law had things moving with case and I didn't have to be at their beckon call like Roby had us.

I called Sunshine Movers and Storage. A place I found online that appeared like a good local company. I planned for them to move my belongings to my new Florida home in the country. Most of my belongings were still in boxes from my previous move when I had to sell my house. My girlfriend that I moved in with had to pack her stuff. But we didn't see any major issues in a move. Boy, did my trusting nature prove I was wrong again.

I didn't do my research on Sunflower Moving and Storage Company out of Kansas City, Kansas. They turned out to be a third-party moving company. The salesperson I talked to on the phone for pricing was talking to me from Chicago. That should have made me suspicious. The move was to take place on Thursday morning. But the loaders called Wednesday evening and said they couldn't be there until Friday. Well, Friday it was calling for rain, that's why I scheduled for Thursday. But at noon Friday, the two Russian loaders that spoke broken English, finally showed up to start loading furniture and other property into a box truck. The truck was like the size Lowe's or Home Depot have, clearly not big enough to put all our property in. He explained that they would load up as much as possible then take it back to the warehouse to unload and return to finish loading the remainder of items. At 0830 on Saturday morning, they finally had finished loading the remaining items while rain came down soaking everything. Then the Russians explained that the salesman had grossly underestimated the number of items they were to load. So, there would be an additional charge. The $6500 quote had grown to $14000.00! Yes, I said $14,000.00 dollars! My call to their office was answered by an Iranian that the loaders said was their mean boss. His demand was for me to pay cash or Post Office Money Orders before they would transport or give me my property. They were holding my property for ransom.

Our belongings were in the hands of thieves and being held for ransom. The power had been shut off that morning because that was what I prearranged with the electric company since we should have been long gone already. It's still raining, I have my pickup loaded a loaded trailer in tow and two dogs and a girlfriend to drive 1100 miles across the country. As if moving two households across the country isn't hard enough. Once again, I was lied to and deceived by people you should be able to trust.

I drove my pickup truck with my girlfriend and two dogs, pulling a U-Haul trailer full of plants and paint that the movers said they couldn't transport. It rained for the first 600 miles as we started our journey. We arrived in Florida two days later to our new to us, empty house. I had arranged for the power to be on before our arrival, so we had lights. But we had no refrigerator, stove, washer, dryer or furniture, but lots of plants. I contacted the Sunflower manager about a delivery time and day. Again, he was very rude, and I could barely understand his broken English with his Farsi accent as he cursed me. The Iranian manager said his name was Sam, laughed and said you might have been told by the salesman your property would be there in three days, but we can hold your property for two weeks if we want. They did. Two weeks later a semi-truck pulled up and two, thirty something Iranians stepped out. In broken English they demanded the $14,000.00 cash or the Post Office Money Orders before they would even open the truck. I said I wanted to see if they really had our things inside before the ransom money was paid. They had given me thousands of reasons to believe they were lying.

I called the Putnum County Sheriffs Office explaining what was going on. In just a few minutes, four Deputies cars had pulled up next to the semi. The Iranian drivers started getting smart with the Deputies and called their boss, Sam, the guy I had spoken to earlier. The driver told him that one of the Deputies was threatening them and even pulled his gun out. One Deputy demanded they open the door before there was any transfer of funds to make sure there was even anything in the truck. They finally complied and opened the rear door. Our stuff was piled high, and I couldn't even see my two motorcycles. But then I had to give them the untraceable Post Office Money Orders they demanded. The Money Orders could only be issued in $1000.00 increments per the local Post Office. Boy, did that cause some attention when I went to purchase them. The lady had never seen that much money change hands in one transaction at her office before.

The Deputies hung around for a bit making sure things were getting unloaded by the drivers. They could tell it was a scam. But told me they couldn't do anything there. They witnessed what was happening and knew these punks worked for a criminal outfit.

The Putnum County Deputies waited for the truck to leave the neighborhood and get back onto State Road 20, where they stopped and pulled them over. The drivers were ticketed for various D.O.T. infractions and their truck was confiscated. They were also taken to jail for outstanding warrants. Thank you, Sherriff Department.

I'm in my seventies now and my day is filled with pain from the time

I wake up until I go to bed. I try not to dwell or think about how I was slighted, betrayed and lied to by so many people I trusted. They cost me thousands of sleepless nights. I still dream on the many gruesome and painful ways I would love to torture and maim the people responsible for my injury and the false representation they willfully conducted. I honestly feel that Blood Eagle on a cross in the Jackson County square is fitting for them for what they did. Rick being the center crucifix, since he likes to play God, with Roby and Nussbeck on each side of him.

Blood Eagle: The ritual allegedly involved carving the victim's back open and cutting their ribs away from their spine, before the lungs were pulled out through the resulting wounds. I so wanted someone besides me to suffer for these many injustices.

CHAPTER 13

THE END?

So, what happened next? A few months past after we got somewhat settled in Florida. I was scheduled to come back to Kansas City for Halls deposition. I had my flight booked and was ready to go. But you guessed it, cancelled. Carter haggled with Hall about the amount that he would pay to keep this out of court. With the million-dollar cap in place as their protection, Hall knew he was protected from any severe harm. That's why that was in place. Attorneys know how to shield themselves within the law. Hall knew he was responsible for Roby's misconduct under his nose and for what he had done to me and the many other clients. Hall knew that he lied to us, and that it had gone on for years. He was just relieved that I was the only one with enough evidence and balls to come after them with proof. All the other victims were so disparaged and out of money thanks to Roby. And they were too disheartened to bring a fight against the law office that was supposed to take care of their problem, not make things worse for them and their families. And where was little Ricky during all this? Hiding like the little punk he has always been. A condescending coward that knows he is wrong but will never admit a fault or take responsibility for what he did. In 70 years, he has never changed. I guess I should have known to never trust him or his judgement. Relationship meant nothing to him.

Carter finally got the hush money up to an amount where he felt that it would be enough to pay for his time and not damage Hall's wallet too much. Everyone wanted to get this case off the books. Even though it should have been front page news, it wasn't the news that lawyers wanted exposed. The fraternity covers for each other so long as they get their cut. I doubt the money was coming from Hall's personal checking account anyway. It would be from the firms stash fund that they kept for "little" misfortunes like this. Remember, Rick made them millions.

Hall finally sent the check over to Carter's office where they took their cut off the top. Then removed more of the winnings for all the expenses incurred during their handling part of this fiasco. Leaving my small percentage of the money that was left over which I would be taxed heavily on for that year. I thought I made very clear to Carter and Stien that I did not want this settlement to be considered income. I had lost way too much in the last six years to give away anymore. But Hall knew what form to file to get his revenge, and Carter accepted it. I was screwed again and wouldn't even know it until later when my tax preparer told me.

And the small little stipend that I got from Tom Stien, my Work Comp lawyer, was equally taxed as income for the year 2022. He got his 25% for his part and I got my little few thousand dollars for a shoulder with 35 percent Partial Permanent Disability. I sure couldn't play golf again or enjoy other activities like playing guitar and drums without pain and restrictions. The thousands of dollars in out-of-pocket money for all the medical, co pays, my pay that was shorted numerous times at Aspen, the pain and suffering for seven years to life was completely discounted by all. I was just an old construction worker that needed to retire. The Second Injury Fund that Roby was going to get me more compensation from was just a phrase that Roby used to make my deal seem sweeter. It did not apply in my case, or that is what Stien said, after I asked him to investigate it.

All the money from the Workman's Compensation settlement and the civil suit against Hall was taxable at 25%. The government said it was all income, thanks to slick Hall. I was able to get the amount owed to the government from the civil case finally reduced to 10%, after I presented documentation that it was a discrimination case. I had never written a check with so many 0's to pay my taxes before.

Now, all the lawyers that had been involved were finally finished with the Scaletty case. Both the civil and work comp cases were settled and over according to them. They had their money up front and had given me my portion of the leftovers. It certainly was not the amount that we discussed back in 2015 when Rick and Roby told me I should have no problem winning this million-dollar case. But Stien felt he did an excellent job of representation after filling Roby's shoes. Jon McCoy and Doug Carter believed they took it to Hall and got me the best deal that was possible with all the roadblocks that Hall tried to throw at them. I still wanted a trial, for if nothing more than for the educating the public about what was happening just a block away from the courthouse. You and I both know the news coverage of an attorney/ conman practicing law just a few blocks from Harry Trumans house would have brought curious viewers. But the fraternity didn't allow that to be exposed.

It was now my turn to stand down, take the settlement, and to go away. Carter said everything that could have been done was done. Carter said he was happy with the settlement. He believed I got a good deal from Hall and that his office did a wonderful job of representing me.

I do not feel that I was treated appropriately, ethically or fairly from the time the accident happened on October 14th, 2014, until the time of settlement. Pat Nussbeck discriminated against me from the time I was injured then increased his despise of me when I challenged him about the truck incident. Nussbeck continued to promote a hostile environment with my coworkers up until the time he could finally fire me. He intentionally shorted and fluctuated my pay and refused to pay me owed out of pocket expenses as he had on all previous jobs. I presented a whole spreadsheet of every pay stub to Roby and Carter that proved it. He covered for his buddy Mario, because he just couldn't admit he failed to properly facilitate the job as I requested. He knew that Mario and his rag tag crew were a terrible excuse for installers, but that's all he had. I was discriminated against by Mario and his workers, who called me "old man" and told other workers that I had 'Oldtimers Disease, "when I reported it, he did nothing. His company was never ready to take on this project with the unskilled idiots provided. Even with the statements from the temp workers that feared for their safety, Aspen didn't care. It just added to another cover up so the client wouldn't know the real status of the job.

My physical therapist lied to me when I first was first sent there by my employer to get treatment. She diagnosed me of just having some arthritis that she could rub out. But finally had to admit after two months of PT that I probably did have a torn rotator cuff. She finally suggested an MRI which proved I was right. The workman's health care is a racket just like the attorney game. Milk the insurance company and the victim for as much as they can.

The list of lies is long when you add them up. I was lied to by Pat Nussbeck countless times. Larry Hadley, the General Manager that recruited me, misleading me with lies of a lucrative career that never happened. He used me as his errand boy and to clean up after his shoddy shingle roofers. Joe Faunce, the other GM that took me away from Hadley to work for him said he had my back. But was too intimidated of Nussbeck and scared of losing his own job to stand up for me. Laura Trotta, the IT gal, was instructed to erase my iPad and everything on it at Nussbeck's order. He saw and knew that the picture documentation I had and still have would be damaging to their agenda and confirming my every charge. Chris Walden, the Commercial Manager that had never installed or supervised a commercial roof, hid quietly under Pats desk. Another big talker with limited experience in any kind of roofing. Even the moving company I trusted took money that I couldn't afford to spare. My first cousin, Rick Scaletty, who lied to me repeatedly during my case, and never investigated the information and charges I gave him about his buddy Roby, and all the crimes he had committed in his office. Roby even bold-faced lied to him, but he was too stupid to recognize it, and bought Roby's bull shit excuses. Why was there so much vindictive behavior from these people. Why were they so conspiring.

My observation during this seven-year ordeal has made me realize that all of them had one common denominator. Surprisingly, every one of them, including my employer, every lawyer involved, judges and doctors that were involved with my case, were all democrats. Did me being a Republican have any bearing? Was my MAGA hat along with my Marine Corps and Stars and Stripes attire I often wore offensive to them? They all did all let me know at various times during our years during this case that they despised Trump. If you're reading this part and it makes you uneasy that I brought this fact to light, maybe you have a little bias in you. See how it works? I had plenty of time to do some investigating and educating myself about this aspect of it and this is what I found out.

Through researching articles on the internet and Google, I have found out that 68% of lawyers are Democrat and 89% of law students today are Democrat. Most colleges today are full of indoctrinated Democrats. Most physicians are as well, as are most roofing company employers. Why do you think that is? I believe because they use the blue-collar workers for their income. They use them like pawns and feel they are easily replaceable. Especially the illegal immigrant workers they get a dime a dozen, especially now with the open wall. They know they can manipulate and steel from them with no legal repercussions. Roofing companies are notorious for this type of activity as are many other employers of illegals and it is more common than you want to know. Rick's own brother-in-law, Tony, a roofing company owner near Kansas City, was arrested and served time for crimes against his illegal immigrant workers. But don't think that the roofing companies don't have lawyers for protection. Aspen has one attorney that takes care of just their conflicts, and he has a busy schedule.

There is a tight fraternity in the lawyer world. They look out for each other and know that their world works behind closed doors. The judges are largely also Democrat and biased, so they work with whatever deal the lawyers have put together. Then behind more closed doors, phone conversations and lunch dates that the client never hears about, they make a backroom deal and let you in on it later to make you feel like you actually played a hand in the negotiations.

It's a money game and the lawyers are always going to come out on top. Never the client or the employee that was injured due to the employer's negligence or their faulty equipment. The little guy suffers because they don't care. You're just another number on the books.

Here's the way they secretly screw you. Law firms and insurance companies use A.I. software and have for decades. It's called Colossus, or Clio. They use this to lower the amount that they would have to pay. Insurance Adjusters can set Colossus intentionally to underpay claims typically up to 20%. This software was created by Allstate back in the 1990's to make it easier for the adjusters and lawyers to review cases and assign values to each claim. After the machine would evaluate the claim, it even would tell the real people what to say. The dummies don't even have to think about how to screw you, the machine does it for them. In today's world there are several claims evaluation software programs. Colossus being the most popular along with ClaimIQ and Claims Outcome Advisor. They are all built after the Colossus model and made to achieve the same goal, to short the injured party the best way they can. I'm sure you have noticed how enormous and shiny those insurance office buildings are. How many commercials do you see on T.V. by injury attorneys now? Every other one is trying to get you to sue so that they can make more money and a better commercial. It's a huge racket setup to discount the injured victim and to make them and their other lawyer friends' money.

This software is not all bad. It can be used for legal calendaring for the law firm. Something greatly needed at the McElligott, Ewan, Hall & Kimminau law office with the great Scaletty and Roby. It would have filled in the court dates, hearings, depositions and task progress. It even tracks billing and hours for the case. A mere software program that could have saved million-dollar Rick's office and his buddy, Roby a lot of problems.

But scuba gear and deep-sea dives are a priority for some. Office efficiency and integrity are down the list evidently.

The algorithms even track the county where the accident happened and looks at recent settlement values for similar cases and recent trial verdicts in the local courts. The insurance companies and lawyers work together to screw you. That's what I've said all along and have now proved it.

The insurance companies share this data with one another, which gives them an advantage against your attorney and you the victim. Don't worry, your lawyer will get his money regardless of the outcome or they wouldn't have taken the case. The lawyers and insurance companies will always have an advantage over you and will use whatever intelligence they can against you.

Now you have read the actions and events that has made me so furious about the way I was treated during this whole process. And what happened to the guilty? Well, let's recap. Mario the Mexican is still attempting construction as a sub-contractor. He runs his enterprise out of his house in KCK. I'm sure with the recent influx of illegals he has a huge base for employees. Larry Hadley suffered an injury at Aspen and received the same retaliation I received. They discounted the severity of his injury, and he went through hell during his recovery process just trying to get resolve. He no longer works for Aspen. Kate, my sneaky secretary, has since left Aspen. I'm sure wherever she is employed she is working her way to the top by stabbing in the back any one in her way. She got away frequently with all kinds of illegal activity altering pay documents and co conspiring with her husband, a salesman for Aspen, to falsify paperwork and receipts that would increase his commissions and payouts. Pat knew, he signed off on them. They have since divorced and neither work for Aspen. The two ladies that were office employees of Aspen, that contacted me after they found out I had a lawsuit, they were hung out to dry by Roby. He never contacted them about their discrimination and wrongful termination that they suffered by Nussbeck at Aspen. I imagine Roby notified Nussbeck giving him a heads up after I gave him the information. They ended up getting screwed like the many others that worked there. Pat Nussbeck is still fills his company with walk ins off the street and training them how to use the insurance system to his company's advantage. I imagine he is still using intimidation against his employees and vendors. He avoided a lengthy jury trial that would have cost him time and money. Roby was instrumental in that and keeping Nussbeck out of court. Bill Hall paid me off the least amount he could get away with to shut me up and not make this public. He is an idiot that let a con man conduct business out of his office for over five years right under his nose. Rick Scaletty is still in hiding either in a foreign country or his mansion in Lakewood. He still has his web site up as KCAttorney.com but doesn't practice anymore. He never really did very much law work after his one big win two decades ago. He did sue his sister a few years ago for some money she owed him for their mother's headstone. Carrie, my ex-wife, has moved back to Olathe, Kansas. She was forced to endure some real bull shit from Roby that she never asked for or deserved. He owes her a huge apology for what he put her and my family through, but we know that will never happen. Her daughter has recently divorced and lives with her along with her grandson.

Roby still lives in Buckner, Missouri with his wife and two boys. After getting disbarred, he picked up a job selling Chief's Superbowl t-shirts out of a tent on a corner in Independence. He has since slightly improved his job status and works at a concession stand at Royals Stadium, if you're looking for him. A loser selling hot dogs for the worst team in the MLB. Fitting!

And where did the payoff money go? Your guess is as good as mine. But I believe from observation, that Roby was making side deals to keep Aspen safe from any large loss. That explains why he sat in my 14 hour of deposition and never made a peep. That also explains why he made frequent trips to the restroom, to powder his nose? Or maybe the money went to wine and dine the various women that I witnessed him return with back to the law office parking lot. I observed him while I sat in my vehicle, early for my 1:00 meetings. He seemed happy with the women, as it always parted with a kiss and hug. My guess was that they were not clients, more he was the client. Or more than likely, Roby was that much of a dumb ass. He had mental issues and things going on that no one picked up on for over five years. Not his best friend, Rick. Not his boss, Bill Hall. Not anyone in the whole judicial system that he worked in daily for 10 years. But what do I know? I'm just the injured worker.

Were Hall and the other flunkies at that law office that incredibly stupid? Why would they let Roby walk around aimlessly in their office for over five years with little or no billable hours of actual work? Hall and Rick were both were too caught up in their own conceited minds to recognize the fraud happening daily in front of them. What worthless failures of human excrement that are directly responsible for the pain caused with many clients and their families.

And me, what am I doing now? Well, I have since relocated to the deep forest of Florida. I discussed earlier why I left KC. At the end of a long sand road sits my doublewide. Inside are my girlfriend and an aggressive dog. You'll see my 30' flagpole flying the Stars and Stripes with the Gadsen flag underneath, and my Trump flag flying proudly on the barn. Take serious note to the Dead End and No Trespassing signs on the way in, they mean what they say. It's quiet out there in the forest. The only sounds are my firearms stinging their targets during the day and the coyote howls at night.

I live in constant pain from my injuries and thought writing this book might distract me for a short time to relieve some of the pain and anger I will forever feel in my body and heart. I'm mad that I was forced into retirement by a greed. That I could have worked until I was 67 and buildup my Social Security and my Union Pensions that I had to withdraw early. How much was that loss? Nobody cares.

I live in peace now but hope the guilty I have mentioned in this book never cross my path in life again. May they die a slow and agonizing death and pray that God condemns their souls for all the sins they have committed during their lucrative and corrupt careers.

I hope you found this book educational and a little bit entertaining. And that you learned from reading about my experience not to trust attorneys, the legal system or that your employer ever has your best interest. You need to take care of yourself and your family's interest first at all costs. If you are injured, harassed, or are experiencing unlawful acts against you by your employer, document, document! I can't stress that enough how important that will be later as your case progresses. Watch your back and remember, coworkers are only that, coworkers. They are not your friends or buddies, just work associates, and they won't have your back when their job is on the line.

I truly appreciate you allowing me to tell the story that cost me my wife, my career, my savings and much of my retirement. The carelessness, arrogance and greed of others almost cost me my life. But it defiantly changed me!

I wonder if anyone that I mentioned in this book wants to sue me for liable or slander? Just remember, I have many boxes full of documentation, pictures, tapes, emails, letters and more containing all the facts I would ever need to prove that everything I have said in this book is true and accurate. You know exactly what you did to me and the others, and know I have the documentation and proof.

I would love to finally have my day in court that I was never allowed to have and to present the evidence that many were too scared to face or defend. Because I assure you, next time there won't be another Injustice Under the Law.

Printed in the United States
by Baker & Taylor Publisher Services